Debt
has a gun to my head

Sanish Shrestha

DEDICATED TO THOSE IN DEBT AND
YOUR FUTURE FINANCIAL FREEDOM

CONTENTS

INTRODUCTION

Universality of debt in modern society

Debt is a ubiquitous entity in today's world, a silent partner in the lives of many, whispering promises of fulfilled desires and future financial freedom. The universality of debt in modern society is both a testament to our advancements and a mirror reflecting our unbridled wants and perceived needs. This book, "Debt has a gun to my head," aims to unravel my dense web of emotions, stress, and psychology surrounding the concept of debt, an exploration not merely of its presence but of its profound impact on my mind, body, and life.

Debt, in its countless forms, impacts individuals from varied socio-economic backgrounds, nations, and cultures. It is not confined by borders or societal norms. From the young graduate shackled by student loans to the entrepreneur navigating through business loans, and the family ensconced in mortgage payments, debt speaks a universal language. It is not merely a financial concept but a social phenomenon, ingrained in the fabric of our modern existence.

The world's economic structure has embraced debt as a crucial component. It facilitates growth, fuels aspirations, and seemingly grants access to unattainable realms. Economies are lubricated by the constant flow of borrowed money, and individuals find solace in the immediate gratification that debt-procured acquisitions provide. This intertwining of prosperity and indebtedness has led to the

1

normalization of debt in our day-to-day lives. It's the looming shadow behind purchases and the relentless whisper accompanying life's choices, affecting decisions and shaping destinies.

Yet, while debt proliferates seemingly unbounded, it concurrently weaves a complex tapestry of stress, anxiety, and psychological turmoil. The incessant worry about repayment, the anxiety surrounding escalating interest, and the guilt of accumulated debts, all form an emotional labyrinth. This intricate interplay between the material and the mental realm renders debt not just an economic concern but a significant psychological and emotional burden.

In a world overwhelmed by consumerism and instant gratification, the concept of 'living within one's means' is continually challenged. Societal and peer pressures, coupled with aggressive marketing strategies, fuel desires, pushing individuals towards a relentless pursuit of more. It is this very pursuit, painted with the hues of modern-day aspirations and framed by societal expectations, that leads to the entrapment within the vicious cycle of borrowing and owing.

The omnipresence of debt also shadows the societal perspective on success and happiness. Acquisitions and material possessions are often perceived as yardsticks for accomplishment and contentment, reinforcing the allure of borrowing. However, beneath this façade of prosperity lies the silent turmoil of sleepless nights, strained relationships, and compromised well-being. The societal view of debt is imbued with paradoxes; it is both a symbol of affluence and a harbinger of stress and anxiety.

This book intends to delve into the multi-dimensional nature of debt, exploring its origins, its evolution, and its undeniable impact on our minds and lives. Through this exploration and my experiences, we seek to understand the psychology behind borrowing, the emotional ramifications of being in debt, and the societal implications of a debt-ridden life. It aims to unmask the silent struggles, reveal the concealed anxieties, and shed light on the untold stories of those living in the shadows of debt.

Moreover, this journey is not just about understanding and empathizing; it is also about learning and evolving. It's about unraveling the strategies to navigate through the quagmire of debt, to break free from its chains and to forge a path towards financial freedom and mental peace. It's about instigating conversations, altering perspectives, and fostering a community of support and knowledge.

The chapters that follow will unfold the multifaceted world of debt, discussing its history, its modern traps, and the ways it affects our health, relationships, and life choices. Personal narratives, expert insights, and research findings will intertwine to provide a holistic view of debt and its implications. We will also explore the road to resilience, prevention, and hope, encouraging each one of us to reclaim our financial destinies.

In the universality of debt, there is a shared struggle, a common ground of experiences and emotions. By delving deep into the heart of debt and its repercussions, this book seeks to create a space of understanding, acceptance, and empowerment, prompting reflections, inspiring changes, and fostering a renewed sense of control and hope in the seemingly relentless grip of debt.

My Journey through the Vortex of Debt

Every word inscribed in this book reverberates with the echoes of my personal odyssey, a journey ensnarled in the intricate webs of debt, marred by silent battles with mounting anxiety, and ultimately, a relentless pursuit of emancipation from financial shackles. My narrative is not just an amalgamation of cold, hard numbers or complex financial terminologies; it's a canvas painted with lived experiences, reflections, and the many emotions and lessons spawned in the labyrinth of debt.

My initial dance with debt commenced at the tender age of 15 or 16 when I acquired my first credit card, co-signed by my grandmother. I had been well-schooled in the prudent utilization of credit. The principle was clear: use it, then promptly clear it. This axiom resonated with me, and in the nascent stages, I adhered strictly to it. However, the specter of lifestyle creep in college permeated my financial life, leading to periods of prolonged debt, fueled by desires for luxuries and vacations.

Embarking on my career with a respectable salary of $46K annually right out of college, I felt a sense of financial freedom and autonomy that was both exhilarating and dangerously misleading. Residing in a city with a pulsating heart like San Francisco, where the cost of living perennially jousts with one's financial stability, my first encounters with substantial financial earnings turned into a dual with my burgeoning desires and the stark reality of bills and responsibilities. My student loans alone were devouring $300 a month, yet the illusion of affluence created by that very first professional paycheck seemed to camouflage the practicality of financial management.

The need of immediate gratification began to overshadow the logical understanding of monetary responsibility. I found myself being seduced by the instant pleasure of acquiring new possessions, be it technology, vacations, or lifestyle upgrades, despite knowing the importance of prioritizing my existing financial obligations like student loans and basic living costs. A shiny new motorcycle, tantalizing vacations to destinations that were whispered into my ears by captivating social media posts, and numerous impulsive decisions propelled by flashy advertisements and peer pressures, swiftly became my financial Achilles heel.

As I glided through the vortex of unbridled spending, my credit card became both a weapon and a shield, enabling me to momentarily satiate my desires while concurrently burying me further into a pit of debt. Each purchase, while offering a transient dopamine surge, was gradually crafting a chain of financial burden that would soon become an omnipresent cloud, quietly overshadowing every aspect of my life and decisions. My habits turned into a cyclical monster; paying my bills, acquiring new things on debt, and satisfying other financial obligations, only to plunge back into the spending spree once again, perpetually feeding the beast of indebtedness.

This continuous spiral was not merely a pathway through various material acquisitions but also an emotional and psychological journey through the highs of possession and the lows of financial strain. It became evident that the transient joy derived from these purchases was swiftly overshadowed by the persistent anxiety of the looming debt that was steadily accumulating. It was a bitter truth that, at the time, was conveniently masked by the temporary exhilaration of every new purchase.

Thus, my journey through the vortex of debt was not merely a numerical or financial spiral; it was intricately woven with emotional, psychological, and social threads that depicted a rich tapestry of experiences, learnings, and realizations, all of which steadily coalesced into a transformative understanding of wealth, possessions, happiness, and ultimately, financial peace. This narrative thus seeks not only to delineate a personal financial journey but also to unveil the deeply entrenched emotional and social aspects that so intricately entwine our experiences with money, debt, and the incessant pursuit of happiness and fulfillment.

Now, on the brink of a new chapter as I prepare to get married, the weight of over $30K of debt is a relentless presence, a silent tormentor gnawing at my mental peace. It's like a gun to my head, compelling me to delve deeper into work, pushing my limits to clear this mountain before my nuptials. The journey is fueled by a resolve to not let my decisions overshadow the life of my partner-to-be. I want to embark on this new journey on a clean slate, unburdened by the chains of past financial choices.

This book is a passage through my life's chapters marked by financial entanglements, a sojourn through the terrains of obligations and repayments, and a reflection on the silent struggles and the whispered lessons. It's a delve into the emotional and psychological ramifications of being in debt, an exploration of the silent sacrifices and the unvoiced anxieties, and a discourse on emerging from the shadows of debt to embrace a life of tranquility and financial stability.

Through the tapestry of my experiences, reflections, and learnings, I aspire to illuminate the human facets of debt, those painted with emotions, reflections, and lived experiences. This book is not just an exposition; it's a dialogue, an invitation to a community of shared understandings and collective learning, and a beacon lighting the path to a life marked by financial freedom and mental peace.

In sharing the various slices of my journey—including my hopes, battles, and reflective moments—I aspire not only to carve out a sanctuary of empathy, understanding, and collective encouragement but also to pave a path toward resolving my own financial and emotional entanglements with debt. Through unearthing and discussing these experiences and insights, I am embarking on a quest to reconquer not just fiscal control, but also a tranquility of mind from the ever-looming specter of debt. It is my earnest belief that as we delve together into these narratives, we can navigate through the intricate webs of financial and emotional turmoil, aiding one another in reclaiming our mental peace and fortifying our paths towards a stable financial destiny.

Purpose of the Book

The genesis of this book lies in a journey—one marked with silent struggles, unspoken anxieties, and relentless battles against the omnipresent shadows of debt. But more than a mere recounting of personal experiences and struggles with debt, the purpose of this book is multifaceted, aiming to serve as a beacon of knowledge, a mirror of reflections, and a catalyst for change.

1. Educational Resource:
This book endeavors to educate its readers about the multifaceted impacts of debt, unraveling its intricate layers and shedding light on its far-reaching repercussions on our lives. It is not merely about understanding the financial implications but delving deeper into my psychological, emotional, and social ramifications of living under the constant weight of financial obligations.

2. Personal Reflection:
Through the lens of my personal journey, marked by continual thoughts of debt every passing minute, this book offers a genuine insight into the lived experiences and silent battles that accompany financial indebtedness. It is a transparent reflection on the effects of debt, not just on one's financial stability but on mental peace, aspirations, relationships, and overall well-being.

3. Universal Resonance:
While centered around personal experiences, the book resonates with the universal experiences of countless individuals ensnared in the web of debt. It aims to be a voice for the silent whispers of many, reflecting the shared struggles, common anxieties, and collective hopes of those striving to navigate through the quagmire of debt.

4. Raise Awareness:
Beyond mere understanding, the book seeks to raise awareness about the pervasive presence of debt in our lives. It strives to initiate conversations, foster discussions, and encourage reflections on the ubiquity of debt in modern society and its implications on our mental, emotional, and social fabrics.

5.   Empowering Change:

Ultimately, the book is a catalyst—a means to empower its readers to reclaim control over their financial destinies. It aspires to ignite a sense of agency and inspire informed, mindful decisions that pave the way towards financial freedom and mental serenity.

6.   Community Building:

By sharing stories, reflections, and learnings, the book endeavors to build a community of empathy, support, and shared knowledge. It aims to foster a space where experiences are validated, understandings are enriched, and collective wisdom is harnessed to navigate the path out of debt.

7.   Promote Mental Well-being:

The intertwined relationship between debt and mental health is a focal point of the discussions in this book. It strives to highlight the mental toll of debt and emphasize the importance of mental well-being in the journey towards financial freedom.

This book, therefore, is not just a narrative. It's a mission—a mission to enlighten, to reflect, to connect, to empower, and to inspire. It's a journey from the shadows of relentless worry into the light of knowledge, empowerment, and peace. It's a call to action, a prompt to introspect, and a guide to navigating the challenging terrains of debt with resilience, awareness, and hope.

Encouraging Readers to Approach Debt with Understanding and Strategy

Navigating through the intricate and often turbulent waters of debt, it's imperative to focus on not only its fiscal implications but also on its pervasive impact across various facets of our lives. The journey, particularly my own expedition through the realm of consumer debt, isn't merely a tale of figures and fiscal strategy, but a more intimate story of wrestling with a looming, oppressive force that often felt like a relentless headache, perpetually holding a metaphorical gun to my head. While the prosperous and affluent might have the liberty to manipulate debt as a tool to strategically augment their wealth, individuals like me, who do not possess a similar financial cushion, perceive and experience debt quite differently. It isn't a tool to be wielded, but an encumbrance to be shed.

Your invitation to traverse this narrative is not merely an invitation to comprehend numbers and strategies; it's an encouragement to delve deeper into an understanding of the multidimensional impacts of debt. It's an exploration into its silent emotional and psychological tremors and a revelation of its invisible influences upon our everyday lives. Perceiving debt should not be regarded as an immovable obstacle but rather acknowledged as a challenge that can be surmounted with comprehensive knowledge, pragmatic strategy, and unyielding resilience.

Each ensuing page of this narrative endeavors not only to educate but to empower you, providing the means to not merely navigate but potentially liberate oneself from the burdensome yoke of financial obligations. Insight is invariably the precursor to empowerment. When armed with knowledge, we are bestowed with the capacity to make informed decisions, construct viable strategies, and traverse our fiscal journey with a restored sense of confidence and clarity.

Developing a strategy, in turn, acts as our steadfast compass amidst the often-treacherous terrains of financial commitments, enabling us to chart a course that thoughtfully allocates resources and efficiently manages our various financial obligations. It becomes our lighthouse, piercing through the foggy journey toward financial solvency and mental tranquility.

Let us, therefore, embark upon this journey in tandem, fortified with a determination to comprehend, a pledge to strategize, and a shared hope to transition from the ominous shadows of debt into the reassuring light of financial liberty and mental peace. Together, let's pave a path forward with shared wisdom, collective strength, and reciprocal support, propelling ourselves toward a future that is unshackled from the binding chains of debt.

A BRIEF HISTORY OF DEBT

Origins of Debt and its Evolution

Debt is an ancient concept, intertwined with the fabric of human societies since their inception. To understand the omnipresence of debt in modern lives, it's crucial to trace its evolution through the annals of history. The origin of debt is symbiotic with the dawn of human civilization, even before the invention of money. It's been an integral component shaping societies, cultures, and economic structures throughout centuries.

The earliest forms of debt did not involve currency but were based on informal agreements and trust within small communities. Early human societies operated mainly on a system of reciprocity and mutual exchange of goods and services—more commonly known as bartering. This barter system was fundamental yet fraught with complications. It relied heavily on the coincidental wants, limiting trade opportunities and making the valuation of goods and services highly subjective and inconsistent. This system laid the rudimentary foundation for debt as it represented an implicit promise of future repayment, either in goods or services.

As societies became more complex, so did their economic structures. The barter system evolved, and more sophisticated methods of trade and credit were developed. The first civilizations in Mesopotamia recognized the necessity for a more standardized form of trade and credit system. They institutionalized the concept of debt, enshrining it in legal codes and documenting it in written records. In ancient civilizations, debt was deeply interwoven with societal norms and often carried religious and moral implications. It was not just an economic construct but was intrinsically linked with the moral and ethical fabrics of the society.

The role of debt in ancient civilizations was multifaceted. It facilitated trade and economic activities, allowing for the accumulation of wealth and the expansion of empires. However, it also became a tool of control and oppression, often leading to servitude and societal inequalities. It was a double-edged sword, a catalyst for growth and development on one hand and a harbinger of inequality and servitude on the other.

Transitioning into the modern era, the face of debt has undergone transformative changes, adapting to the evolving economic landscapes and societal needs. The introduction of credit cards, mortgages, and student loans marked significant milestones in the trajectory of debt. These instruments expanded the accessibility of credit, enabling a broader spectrum of the population to leverage debt for varied purposes, such as education, home ownership, and consumption.

In contemporary societies, debt has become a pervasive phenomenon, embedded in almost every aspect of our lives. The shift from tangible assets to digital transactions has profound implications. The digitalization of money and transactions has facilitated the seamless integration of debt into our daily lives, making it more accessible and, concurrently, more invisible. This invisibility cloaks the real impact of debt, allowing it to permeate our lives subtly, impacting our decisions, behaviors, and well-being.

The implications of this shift are manifold. The ease and convenience of digital transactions mask the accumulating obligations, often leading to over-reliance and over-extension of credit. The invisibility of digital debt exacerbates the psychological stress and anxiety associated with financial obligations, as the tangible reminder of debt becomes obscured in the sea of numbers and transactions. Furthermore, the seamless amalgamation of debt in digital transactions fuels consumerism, pushing individuals towards unsustainable financial behaviors and choices.

The evolution of debt from its rudimentary forms in ancient civilizations to its sophisticated structures in modern societies reflects the changing economic landscapes and societal norms. The transformation of debt, from tangible assets to digital transactions, echoes the shifts in our perceptions, attitudes, and interactions with financial obligations. It's a journey marked by advancements and regressions, opportunities, and exploitations, growth, and inequalities.

Understanding the origins and evolution of debt is instrumental in comprehending its pervasive presence in our lives today. It provides insights into the multifaceted nature of debt, shedding light on its impacts, its influences, and its implications on our societies, our behaviors, and our well-being. The journey through the annals of debt is not just a historical exploration but a philosophical reflection on our relationships with money, obligations, and each other. The tapestry of debt's history is woven with threads of human aspirations, struggles, innovations, and moralities, reflecting the complexities of human societies and their incessant pursuit of growth, development, and equity.

Bartering to Credit Systems

The transition from bartering to credit systems marks a pivotal point in economic history, transforming the way societies operate, trade, and evolve. The change reflects the constant human endeavor to overcome the limitations of existing systems and to create structures that cater to the evolving needs and complexities of societies.

The Limitations of Bartering:
Bartering, the initial method of trade, was based on a simple exchange of goods and services. It was a system of direct reciprocity, governed by the mutual needs of the parties involved. However, bartering had its limitations. It was constrained by the "coincidence of wants," meaning it could only occur if two parties had the exact opposite needs at the same time, a condition seldom met.

The Advent of Money:
To overcome the limitations of bartering, ancient civilizations introduced money as a medium of exchange—a universally accepted intermediary in trade transactions, allowing for more fluidity and flexibility in trade. Money acted as a standardized measure of value, making trade more consistent and widespread. It served as a store of

value, a unit of account, and a medium of exchange, eliminating the reliance on the coincidence of wants and paving the way for more complex economic structures.

Evolution to Credit Systems:

With the advent of money, the evolution to credit systems was a natural progression. Credit systems allowed transactions to occur even if one party did not have the immediate means to pay, promising future payment. This system allowed for the expansion of trade and economic activities, enabling individuals and societies to plan, invest in ventures, and accumulate wealth. The introduction of credit marked the beginning of debt as we understand it today, with its implications and complexities.

The Role of Trust and Institutions:

Credit systems inherently relied on trust—trust that the debtor would fulfill their promise of future payment. As societies grew and transactions became more complex and widespread, informal trust-based systems were no longer sufficient. Formal institutions were established to regulate, document, and enforce credit agreements. These institutions played a crucial role in the development and stabilization of credit systems, mitigating risks, and fostering economic growth.

The Development of Modern Credit:

Over centuries, credit systems have continuously evolved, adapting to the changing needs, technologies, and complexities of societies. The introduction of banking systems, credit cards, and various lending instruments have revolutionized the accessibility and utilization of credit. These modern credit systems have allowed for unparalleled economic growth, innovation, and individual empowerment. However, they have also brought forth new challenges, including economic inequalities, over-reliance on credit, and the psychological implications of debt.

Implications:

The journey from bartering to modern credit systems highlights the dynamic evolution of economic structures and human societies. This evolution has been marked by human ingenuity, adaptability, and the incessant pursuit of progress. While the progression from bartering to credit has unlocked unprecedented opportunities and advancements, it has also woven the fabric of debt tighter around our lives, impacting our behaviors, decisions, and well-being.

The transformation of economic systems from the simplicity of barter to the complexity of modern credit is a mirror reflecting the multifaceted evolution of human civilizations. It is a narrative of progress and challenges, of opportunities and risks, of empowerment and dependence. Understanding this transformation is instrumental in navigating the intricate landscapes of debt and credit in our contemporary world, allowing us to approach them with informed perspectives, strategic insights, and mindful reflections.

Debt's Role in Ancient Civilizations

Debt has played a significant and multifaceted role in the fabric of ancient civilizations. It was a concept intertwined with societal structures, economic systems, ethical considerations, and often religious beliefs. Its role was not merely confined to economic transactions but extended to the core principles and values governing societies.

1. Economic Mechanism:

In ancient civilizations, debt acted as a crucial economic mechanism facilitating trade and commercial activities. It enabled the allocation and distribution of resources, allowing societies to plan, develop, and prosper. The formalization of debt agreements allowed for the accumulation of wealth, enabling the undertaking of large-scale projects and advancements in infrastructure, agriculture, and technology.

The potent role of debt in the historical context is vividly illustrated by the Mesopotamian society, notably during the Babylonian period. The Code of Hammurabi, established around 1754 BC, represents one of the earliest and most comprehensive legal codes related to debt and financial management. This set of laws not only regulated personal loans and credit but also enabled large-scale economic and infrastructural developments by formalizing debt agreements. The societal and economic framework of Babylon, thus, was significantly shaped by these legal codifications of debt, which delineated clear rules for loans, interest rates, and defaults.

In practical terms, Mesopotamian society utilized this structured debt system to facilitate both individual and state-level endeavors. Temples and palace complexes, being the dominant economic centers, managed and extended credit, enabling advancements like the construction of monumental Ziggurats and extensive irrigation projects. Silver, measured by weight, and detailed cuneiform tablets facilitated these sophisticated financial transactions in the absence of coin money, thereby ensuring a regulated distribution of resources and funding for substantial projects, which in turn propelled societal progression and economic prosperity.

2. Social Structure and Class Division:

Debt was a defining factor in the social structures and class divisions in ancient societies. It often led to the creation of hierarchical systems where debtors were subjugated by creditors. The inability to repay debts could result in servitude or enslavement, perpetuating inequalities and affecting the dynamics of power and privilege within societies.

A palpable example underscoring the potent impact of debt on social structures and class divisions unfurls in Ancient Rome. Here, debt was deeply entrenched in the societal fabric, invariably influencing the power dynamics between different strata of society. The Roman Empire, with its complex socioeconomic system, had a stark dichotomy between the affluent patricians and the less affluent plebeians. Debt would often spiral into a formidable force, dictating the life trajectories of the plebeians, who, when encumbered by unpayable debts, would find themselves ensnared in a system known as "nexum". This allowed a debtor to become a bonded servant, or "nexus", when they were unable to fulfill their financial obligations. The exploitation and subjugation of these debtors permeated the societal structure, etching deep-rooted divisions and perpetuating a cycle where the wealthy creditor class wielded significant power and influence over the debtor class, ensuring a perpetuation of inequality and hierarchal subjugation.

Moreover, this cyclical bondage to debt not only maintained existing social hierarchies but also often restricted social mobility, solidifying class structures. The nexum system created an environment where the creditor class could exploit the labor and services of the indebted, further amplifying their wealth and societal standing. Conversely, the debtor class, entrenched in their financial obligations, found it exceedingly difficult to ascend the social ladder. Thus, the pivotal role of debt as both a facilitator and a barrier in the social and economic realms of Ancient Rome weaves a compelling tale of its intricate and multifaceted impacts on society, showcasing a complex interplay between financial structures, social mobility, and power dynamics.

3. Legal and Ethical Frameworks:

The concept of debt necessitated the establishment of legal frameworks and ethical norms to govern transactions and relationships. In ancient Mesopotamia and Rome, for instance, laws were formulated to regulate debt contracts, interest rates, and repayment conditions. These legal codifications were reflections of the moral and ethical paradigms of the time, often entwining debt with notions of justice, righteousness, and societal obligations.

In ancient Rome, legal norms around debt were robustly formalized through the Twelve Tables, a codification that was prominently engraved in the sociopolitical life of the republic. Debt and its implications were diligently managed, with stipulations that addressed issues of borrowing and lending, ensuring equitable practice and safeguarding societal order. For example, under the Twelve Tables, if a debtor failed to repay a debt within 30 days of it being due, they could be seized by the creditor, brought before a magistrate, and if the debt was verified, they could either repay it immediately or be placed in bondage. The legal frameworks related to debt in both ancient Mesopotamia and Rome did not merely serve as transactional guidelines; they were emblematic of a deeply rooted ethical narrative that sought to ensure justice, equality, and moral integrity in financial dealings, concurrently steering societal behavior and norms. This, in turn, infused debt with a moral and ethical weight, steering it beyond a mere economic instrument to one that was woven into the broader tapestry of societal and moral norms.

4. Religious Implications:

In many ancient civilizations, debt was intertwined with religious beliefs and practices. It was perceived through the lens of moral and spiritual obligations. For example, in several ancient cultures, the remission of debts was seen as a divine mandate, and periodic debt forgiveness was practiced as a religious principle to maintain societal harmony and moral order.

Diving into the historical landscape of ancient civilizations, the intersection of debt and religion is palpably evident, highlighting the profound spiritual implications of economic interactions. A striking instance is found in the practice of the "Jubilee Year" within ancient Hebrew society, as delineated in the Biblical Book of Leviticus. This tradition, meant to occur every 50th year, declared the forgiveness of debts, emancipation of slaves, and the return of lands to their original owners. Rooted in the religious principle of ensuring equality and preventing enduring poverty, the Jubilee Year was not merely an economic practice but a profound reflection of spiritual and ethical commitments, demonstrating how economic actions such as debt forgiveness were entwined with deeper spiritual and ethical imperatives.

In a parallel vein, ancient Sumer, located in the southernmost region of Mesopotamia, demonstrated a similar intertwining of debt and religious practice through the institution of the "amargi," the Sumerian term translating to 'return to the mother,' which was essentially a proclamation that allowed those enslaved due to debt to return home. Notably, it was also employed in the broader sense to denote general debt cancellation. These regular debt cancellations were deeply ingrained within both the economic and spiritual life of Sumerian society, reflecting a holistic approach that recognized the indispensability of maintaining a balanced societal structure through the religiously-infused practice of debt remission. Thus, debt, in these contexts, transcended its economic functionality, embedding itself within the spiritual and ethical bedrock of society, mirroring a comprehensive understanding of economic stability as being innately bound to societal and spiritual well-being.

5. Political Tool:

Debt served as a powerful political tool, allowing rulers and elites to control resources, influence policies, and maintain power. It was used strategically to solidify alliances, impose tributes, and manage internal and external relationships. The manipulation of debt was instrumental in shaping the political landscapes and trajectories of ancient civilizations.

Immersing ourselves in the intricate tapestry of historical politics and economics, it becomes transparent that debt has always woven a path through the echelons of power and control, notably acting as a prominent instrument in the arsenal of political machinations throughout myriad civilizations. For instance, the Roman Empire, with its vast territories and nuanced political structures, illustrates a compelling exemplar. Here, debt was astutely wielded as a mechanism to fortify the allegiance of provincial rulers and elite classes. High-ranking Romans would extend loans to provincial leaders, intertwining them in a web of financial obligation that served to concurrently assure loyalty to the Roman polity while maintaining a semblance of autonomy among the subjected territories.

In another illustration, ancient China's imperial rulers utilized debt strategically to control the agrarian economy, implementing a granary system that allowed farmers to borrow in times of need and repay with harvested crops, securing a pivotal role for the state in both economic sustenance and creating a dependency relationship that was pivotal for maintaining political stability and control. Moreover, this was not merely an economic transaction but a potent political strategy that ensured the subservience and compliance of the agrarian masses, cementing the political authority of the imperial leadership. These instances underscore how debt, with its ability to tether parties in a binding fiscal and sociopolitical dynamic, was not just an economic interaction but a discerning tool deftly manipulated to sculpt the political landscapes of ancient civilizations, illuminating the many roles of debt in shaping historical epochs.

6. Catalyst for Revolts and Reforms:

The burdens of debt and the associated inequalities often led to social unrest, revolts, and demands for reforms in ancient societies. The struggles against debt bondage and the quest for debt forgiveness were recurring themes in the socio-political narratives of antiquity, reflecting the inherent tensions and conflicts surrounding debt.

To fathom the profound ways in which debt became a potent catalyst for upheavals and transformative reforms in ancient societies, we can delve into the palpable unrest that percolated through the stratified social structures of such eras, often culminating in widespread resistance and calls for systemic change. A paradigmatic instance can be gleaned from the Roman Republic, wherein the heavy yoke of debt stirred the seeds of rebellion among the plebeians, ultimately giving rise to the Conflict of the Orders.

Strapped under oppressive debts and with the specter of debt bondage hanging ominously over them, the plebeians sought refuge in collective resistance, eventually extracting significant political concessions, including the inception of the Twelve Tables, a seminal legal code that, among other things, addressed aspects of debt and creditors.

Similarly, the Athenian society of the 6th Century BC was markedly jolted by the waves of discontent and protestations born out of the pervasive inequalities perpetuated by an onerous debt system. Subjugated under the whims of a ruthless aristocracy and beleaguered by the specter of enslavement for unpaid debts, the lower echelons of society became a simmering cauldron of revolt. It was amidst this tumult that Solon, the archetypal Athenian statesman, enacted a series of reforms, famously known as Seisachtheia, or the "shaking off of burdens", liberating many Athenians from the oppressive chains of debt and bondage, and implementing prohibitions against the enslavement for debt. These epochs, among numerous others, vividly illustrate how the complexities of debt and financial bondage invariably became a flashpoint for societal unrest and upheavals, spurring reforms and recalibrations that have indelibly shaped the historical and sociopolitical narratives of ancient civilizations.

The role of debt in ancient civilizations was profound and multifaceted, serving as an economic catalyst, a social determinant, a moral construct, a religious principle, a political instrument, and a source of conflict and transformation. Understanding the diverse roles and implications of debt in ancient societies provides valuable insights into its enduring impact on human civilizations. It allows us to perceive debt not merely as a financial construct but as a complex and dynamic entity shaped by, and shaping, the cultural, ethical, political, and societal dimensions of human existence.

This perspective enables a deeper and more nuanced exploration of the relationships, influences, and tensions between debt and society, enriching our comprehension of its contemporary manifestations and challenges.

Modern-day Debt: Credit Cards, Mortgages, Student Loans

The landscape of debt has evolved dramatically from its ancient iterations, adapting to the complexities of modern economies and the diverse needs of contemporary societies. Today, debt permeates various aspects of our lives, manifesting in forms such as credit cards, mortgages, and student loans. Each of these represents a facet of modern life, reflecting our aspirations, lifestyles, and societal structures.

1. Credit Cards: The Gateway to Consumer Debt:
- Ease and Accessibility: Credit cards symbolize the ease and accessibility of consumer credit in the modern age, allowing individuals to make purchases beyond their immediate financial means.
- Consumerism and Lifestyle: They fuel consumerism and enable lifestyle choices, impacting spending behaviors and financial planning.
- Interest Rates and Revolving Debt: High-interest rates and the nature of revolving debt can lead to accumulating balances and prolonged financial obligations, creating a cycle of indebtedness.
- Psychological Implications: The ease of using credit cards often diminishes the perception of spending real money, leading to overextension and financial stress.
- Credit Building versus Financial Overreaching: While credit cards serve as an effective tool to build and enhance credit scores, pivotal for securing favorable terms on loans and mortgages, this utility often comes tethered to a perilous temptation. The facility to access credit and make deferred payments can potentially entice individuals into a vortex of purchasing beyond their means, gradually sliding into a quagmire of debt. This dichotomy underscores the necessity for prudence and calculated utilization, where the benefits of credit building are harnessed without succumbing to the seductive ease of accumulating debt. A well-navigated strategy that balances judicious spending with timely payments can pave the way towards healthy financial habits, albeit necessitating a conscientious and disciplined approach to circumvent the pitfalls of overleveraging.

2. Mortgages: Homeownership and Financial Stability:
- Path to Homeownership: Mortgages facilitate homeownership, enabling individuals to acquire real estate as a means of establishing stability and building wealth.
- Long-term Commitment: They represent a long-term financial commitment, with implications for individual financial strategies and lifestyle choices.
- Real Estate Market Dynamics: The dynamics of real estate markets and mortgage terms can impact financial security, influencing equity and debt levels.
- Impact on Financial Planning: The significance of mortgage debt necessitates careful financial planning and risk assessment, affecting saving, investment, and consumption decisions.

3. Student Loans: Investing in the Future:
- Access to Education: Student loans open the doors to higher education, enabling individuals to pursue academic and professional aspirations.
- Burden of Repayment: The burden of student loan repayment can be daunting, affecting career choices, lifestyle decisions, and financial well-being.
- Impact on Life Choices: The obligation to repay student loans can influence major life choices, including starting a family, buying a home, and entrepreneurial endeavors.
- Socioeconomic Disparities: The availability and necessity of student loans reflect underlying socioeconomic disparities and access to educational opportunities, influencing social mobility and equity.

4. Digitalization and Invisible Debt:
- Seamless Transactions: The shift to digital transactions makes debt more seamless and invisible, integrating it subtly into daily lives.
- Overextension and Overspending: The invisibility and ease of digital debt often catalyze overextension and overspending, exacerbating financial vulnerabilities. One might easily subscribe to several streaming services for

entertainment and indulge in frequent online shopping sprees to stay abreast of the latest trends, all with just a few effortless clicks and perhaps facilitated by readily accessible credit options. The immediacy and convenience of such transactions can obscure the accruing financial commitment, especially when there is no tangible exchange of money, masking the gradual buildup of substantial financial obligations.

- Behavioral and Psychological Consequences: The psychological and behavioral consequences of invisible debt are profound, affecting stress levels, mental health, and financial behaviors.

- Data Privacy and Security Concerns: With the digitalization of debt comes an escalating concern over the privacy and security of personal and financial data. The ever-present risk of data breaches, phishing, and other cyber-attacks poses not only a threat to financial stability but also adds an additional layer of anxiety and vigilance to the management of digital finances. Individuals must navigate through the convenience of digital transactions while simultaneously safeguarding against potential cybersecurity threats, invariably intertwining financial management with perpetual caution and an imperative for robust digital literacy.

5. Implications and Reflections:
- Pervasiveness of Debt: Modern-day debt is pervasive, influencing various aspects of individual lives and societal structures.

- Behavioral and Societal Impact: The implications of contemporary forms of debt extend beyond financial considerations to behavioral patterns, societal norms, and overall well-being.

- Empowerment and Entrapment: While modern debt empowers individuals by providing access to resources and opportunities, it can also act as a mechanism of entrapment, limiting freedom and inducing stress.

- Strategic Approach and Financial Literacy: Navigating the modern debt landscape necessitates a strategic approach, informed decisions, and enhanced financial literacy to balance empowerment and responsibility.

Grasping the significance and implications of modern-day debt requires us to navigate through the intricate tapestry of its history, unraveling threads that are tightly knit with our aspirations, behaviors, and societal frameworks. The metamorphosis of debt, from its nascent tangible exchanges witnessed in ancient civilizations to today's sophisticated, and often invisibly entwined, financial instruments, offers a compelling narrative of the interaction between evolving human societies and their economic structures. This evolution encapsulates shifts, not only in transactional modalities but also in the philosophical underpinnings and societal perceptions tethered to the concept of owing.

A scrutiny into the historical context elucidates how debt has perennially been more than a mere economic tool; it has concurrently been a psychological and social construct, impacting both individual psyches and societal dynamics. An intimate comprehension of various forms, implications, and influences of debt thus morphs into an essential endeavor, allowing us to better gauge its omnipresence in our contemporary existence. It provides a lens through which we can critically examine and relate to our own financial liabilities and obligations in the modern world.

Engaging with the historical trajectory of debt not only enlightens our understanding of its current complexities but also arms us with a nuanced perspective. It enables individuals and societies to strategically navigate through the labyrinthine world of modern financial obligations. In doing so, it grants us the capability to leverage the opportunities birthed from debt while concurrently developing mechanisms to mitigate its challenges and risks, thereby establishing a balanced, informed, and empowered relationship with it. This interplay between understanding historical contexts and applying insights to contemporary scenarios becomes pivotal in forging pathways towards not just financial literacy and stability, but also towards nurturing healthier mental and societal landscapes in the realm of economic exchanges and obligations.

THE MODERN DEBT TRAP

The allure of "buy now, pay later" and 0% interest

The allure of "buy now, pay later" is nothing less than enchanting, a captivating illusion promising immediate satisfaction with postponed fiscal repercussions. This financial mantra, seemingly revolutionary, transforms into a pitfall: "Broke Now, Broke Later"—an inevitable outcome when we commit future earnings to validate current desires.

"Buy now, pay later" can be seen as an evolution of the once-prominent "0% interest" payment plans, intertwining deferred payment with the absence of immediate financial burden, thereby seamlessly integrating an enticing spending trap into the consumer experience. These offers, waving banners of "no interest if paid in full within 6 months" or "0% APR for 12 months," are meticulously crafted to offer an illusion of financial flexibility and prudence. It seductively beckons consumers into acquiring their desires instantaneously while deferring the monetary impact under a seemingly cost-free umbrella. Though hidden beneath the alluring surface of these plans, the treacherous fine print reveals a future potentiality of skyrocketing interest rates and the looming threat of accumulated back interest, should one misstep and fail to navigate the stipulated repayment timeframe. Thus, what initially masquerades as a financially savvy endeavor can rapidly morph into a precarious plunge into inadvertent debt, illustrating that this evolution in purchasing options harbors a deceptive underbelly, catalyzing a cycle of continual indebtedness whilst operating under a façade of astute financial management.

In the realm of this enchanting purchasing paradigm, I found my journey marred with countless temptations and subtle traps. The echoing sirens of new gadgets and a symbol of enduring love, an engagement ring, momentarily blinded me to the impending financial strains. Small and seemingly manageable commitments like $600 gadgets parsed out over three months seemed innocuous. However, the left-over money from one "buy now, pay later" is used on another "buy now, pay later.", They stealthily tether the budget, shifting funds from elemental needs to fleeting luxuries.

I had been diligently saving for seven to eight years, imagining the sparkle of the perfect engagement ring. The goal was to make a wise and sound investment. With all the money in my hand the gentleman procuring my diamond offered a 12-month, no-interest plan. It looked like a golden opportunity, the $6,000 down payment seemed like a drop in the ocean, and the $1,569 monthly commitment felt like a breeze, especially with my savings tucked safely away. My heart was light, and my dreams were bright. I was going to have a massive emergency fund in the "just case" moments.

Ring in hand, our yearly anniversary destination was unmistakably set: New York. As our 8th anniversary approached, it wasn't just another romantic getaway—it was poised to be the backdrop of our life's next chapter. This milestone, the leap from boyfriend to fiancé, was one we both eagerly anticipated. We've always treasured our anniversary trips, and this tradition, steeped in love and shared experiences, was about to witness its most profound moment. New York, with its electrifying allure and boundless horizons, beckoned as the idyllic setting for this transformative gesture. With tickets secured and excitement brimming, I secretly embarked on a mission—to curate the most unforgettable proposal. Entrusted with designing our journey, I sought to outdo myself, propelled by the 0% interest for 12-month offer on the engagement ring. It subtly bolstered my spending confidence, and soon, our days were dotted with luxuries we hadn't even dreamt of: gourmet feasts, spontaneous adventures, and whimsical indulgences. The funds earmarked for the ring seemed to stretch, becoming a magic key unlocking New York's numerous splendors. My drive to make this expedition unparalleled momentarily blurred the looming fiscal reality. And while every penny spent enhancing her joy remains a choice I'd make again, the shadow of the debt, juxtaposed against our engagement's glow, lingered as a stark reminder of the dues yet to be settled.

After the exhilaration of the proposal and our time in New York began to settle, the reality of my financial commitments surfaced. Every delightful meal we shared, every chuckle under the bright Broadway lights, and every unexpected purchase were now interspersed with the reminders of pending payments. Yet, there was an unwavering conviction within me: the moments of magic we had woven together were worth every cent. While the weight of debt was undeniable and budget recalibrations became a frequent exercise, the happiness of those memories fueled my determination. The challenge lay ahead, not in questioning the worth of our experiences, but in navigating the path to financial equilibrium.

The trap of "buy now, pay later" offers a false promise of immediate satisfaction, allowing us to indulge without the immediate sting of financial burden. This sates our elevated spending appetites and obscures genuine affordability considerations. The illusion of affordability beckons, enticing us to make purchases that our current financial states cannot support. This illusion is a gateway to lifestyle inflation and mounting debts.

Engagements with multiple "buy now, pay later" plans silently gnaw at the monthly budget, with individuals often finding themselves caught in the middle of necessities and indulgences, teetering to maintain financial equilibrium. The financial stresses that follow necessitate lifestyle modifications—liquidating unused possessions, adopting a more frugal life, and perennially reassessing spending habits.

It's clear that those seemingly minor purchases, a camera here, a lens there, and some PC gear, have a way of catching up with you. It's like they silently compile, turning into this monthly ritual of payments, which inevitably start to divert funds from basic necessities.

I found myself in a constant financial hustle, rifling through my belongings to find items to sell and trying to live a bit more sparingly, all because I had allocated my future money to fulfill my current desires. This inflated lifestyle that seemed so attainable was just a façade, masking the true impact of my purchasing decisions. The immediate allure of acquiring what I wanted when I wanted felt intoxicating, but the resulting journey was anything but glamorous.

These financial restrictions and stresses significantly hamper one's ability to pursue future plans and desires, creating a perpetual struggle between the joys of the present and the aspirations of the future. The "buy now, pay later" model inherently binds us to future scarcity, as future incomes are predestined to satiate past expenditures. This model shackles financial freedom, tying individuals to their past financial decisions and inhibiting the realization of their present and future financial potentials. This cycle perpetuates financial stress and limitations, significantly impacting mental well-being and overall life satisfaction.

The psychological repercussions of such a financial model are also profound. The emotional discord between the joy of immediate gratification and the following financial strains results in cognitive dissonance, altering decision-making processes and affecting mental health. This perpetual financial strife induces modifications in financial behaviors, promoting savings, frugality, and a renewed scrutiny of spending habits.

Having the patience to save and then pay with hard, tangible cash brings a level of satisfaction and relief that is unparalleled. It's a subtle acknowledgment of discipline, a nod to financial foresight. The transient euphoria of immediate possession swiftly becomes overshadowed by the prolonged stress and restrictions it imposes. It shackled my desires, turning days into a relentless pursuit to reconcile my past decisions with my present circumstances.

The joy derived from cash payments, free from the chains of future financial commitments, stands unparalleled, bestowing a sense of financial autonomy and freedom. Reflections on the journey through the labyrinth of "buy now, pay later" illuminate the essence of balanced and informed financial planning and the alignment of spending, saving, and investing with one's values and aspirations. The process catalyzes a reevaluation of life choices and values, fostering a more conscious and intentional approach to life and finances.

The charm of "buy now, pay later" is transient and misleading, shadowed by prolonged strains of financial commitments. It's a deceptive pledge to future constraints, prioritizing past indulgences over current needs and future aspirations. My odyssey through this seductive yet treacherous path has been a whirlwind of emotions, financial battles, and transformative lessons. It served as a reflective mirror, revealing my choices, values, and desires, and as an enlightening mentor, emphasizing financial prudence, planning, and the quest for authentic happiness.

My journey, a kaleidoscope of financial interactions, underscored the genuine worth of "Broke Now, Broke Later," where the allure of future money played the pivotal role. The numerous engagements with this financial paradigm, whether it be gadgets parsed into monthly commitments or an engagement ring veiled in a no-interest promotion, highlighted the perils of leveraging future money.

When I succumbed to the temptations of luxury during a vacation to New York, the funds that should have been an auto debit to a savings account morphed into symbols of opulence. The struggle that ensued, where every day became a battle to offset the debts, emphasized the profound implications of such a financial model. The mounting commitments subtly chipped away at my finances, forcing a life of frugality, constantly grappling with the consequences of past purchases, overshadowing the transient joys of immediate gratification.

The concluding realization is stark—the ephemeral joy of immediate acquisitions is a fleeting mirage compared to the enduring satisfaction and freedom derived from a life of financial harmonization, informed choices, and alignment with one's intrinsic values and aspirations. The reflection on this journey unravels invaluable insights and nuances about financial prudence and the pursuit of a fulfilled life, a revelation about the true essence of happiness and contentment.

The consumerist culture and social pressures

Delving into the intricate dance between consumerist culture and social pressures, it's fascinating, and at times, startling, to observe the strings that pull us, almost puppet-like, towards a constant swirl of acquisition and indulgence. It's like living in a never-ending cycle where the eagerness to blend in, to relish in the shared experiences and to momentarily dazzle in the sparkle of possessions, holds our strings, making us dance to the beats of spending, sometimes well beyond our means.

The ethos of consumerist culture is profoundly enshrined in the constant pursuit of more—more possessions, more experiences, more indulgences. It's a world where value is often associated with quantity and possession, where the charm of the new and the allure of the trendy become the parameters defining our worth and our choices. This relentless pursuit, more often than not, goes beyond our means, chaining us to a perpetual cycle of debt and regret.

Consumerist culture, for me, has always been a dance between desire and reality. It's a world where the swift swipe of my American Express can momentarily dissolve the distinctions between me and the influencers of my world. Reflecting on it, I genuinely feel college was the turning point for me, a catapult launching me into the world of new influences and subtle compulsions.

I remember my high school days in Fort Worth, Texas, where my spending was more anchored, more attuned to my personal needs and capacities. My purchases were driven by my earnings, and my transactions were simple debit ones, nothing that lingered or tied me down. But, college in San Francisco, California was a different ball game, a whirlwind of new cultures, trends, and influences, each one silently reshaping my spending habits.

The shift was subtle yet profound. My dorm mates, my classmates, the group of guys I shared a condo with, each had a different allure, a different style that silently beckoned to be emulated. One of my buddies was into shoes—Nikes, Air Jordans—you name it, and somehow, his passion became my pursuit. Before I knew it, I was swiping my card, buying and selling hot releases, hoping against hope that I could balance the scales later.

This whirlwind of influence didn't stop at shoes. A fancy haircut at an upscale salon became another fleeting pursuit, inspired by a friend's new look. For me, the result seemed pretty much the same as my regular $20 cut. But the venture cost me an extra $45, a dent I could have easily avoided.

It's almost like the age-old tale of keeping up with the Joneses. Witnessing something cool that someone had sparked a desire to own the same. It was more than just possession; it became a gateway to shared experiences, shared topics—essentially a medium to blend in, to be a part of the vibrant college tapestry.

The tapestry became more colorful when one of my best friends introduced me to the world of motorcycles. The thrill was real, and soon, I had my own bike, the first one I had bought after meticulously saving up 4K. The initial joy was short-lived as it got stolen, pushing me into the cycle of loans for the next one. I opted not to get comprehensive insurance, so I received nothing from my provider and had to start back on square one. About 2 years later, when I received my first raise at work, I immediately went and got another motorcycle; however, I took out a loan. A bike totaling 10K, 2K down payment and an 8K loan at 5% for a whopping 72 months! The rollercoaster didn't stop there. This one got stolen too a year later, but luckily, I had learned my lesson and had comprehensive insurance.

Caught in the relentless whirl of consumerist culture, the motorcycle loan became a symbol of my financial entanglement, a constant reminder of the persistent deductions that every paycheck would endure. This decision wasn't just a pursuit of thrill and adventure, it was a testament to how deeply ingrained the desire to conform and showcase status had become in my psyche. The appeal of the motorcycle, accentuated by societal norms and peer influence, had nudged me into committing a substantial portion of my future earnings to service this debt, both for the loan and the insurance. The enchantment of possessing a shining symbol of freedom and rebellion made it seem worth the financial strain, but the reality was a monthly cycle of bills eating away at my freedom, rather than enhancing it. This scenario amplified the stress and reinforced the realization that the tangible possessions and lifestyle allurements were temporary, but the financial repercussions were long-lasting and far-reaching. The relentless societal pressures and consumerist propensities had not just encouraged acquisitions but had, more profoundly, entangled me deeper into the intricate web of debt and financial instability.

All these acquisitions, the shoes, the motorcycle, and the other possessions did, and still do, hold significance for me. But the labyrinth of debt it entangled me in made me rethink my priorities. The Instagram hype, the lavish eateries, all seemed to echo the "spend, spend" mantra, pushing me further into the realm of debt. This mindset didn't just stop with material possessions; it extended into my college life too.

Life on campus and the vibrant streets of San Francisco echoed with the enticements of the 'college experience'. Rather than making economical use of my university meal plan, I was often swept up in exploring San Francisco's city dining, enjoying the city's gastronomy with friends. This pursuit of culinary adventures outside the confines of our campus had me neglecting the prepaid University Café Money. As the end of the school year neared, I was hit with the reality of having over $1.5K left in my meal account. This wasn't money I could save or roll over; it was a use-it-or-lose-it system. Despite my last-minute attempts to splurge within the campus café, it was evident I had wasted a significant portion of what I'd borrowed. That lingering sum became a glaring reflection of my financial oversight and the need to strike a balance between enjoying the college life and managing funds judiciously.

The dance with consumerism didn't end with college. It morphed into newer forms, driven less by the need to impress and more by the desire to experience. Fancy bars, streaming video games, exotic vacations—all became avenues to savor life, to experience the vibrancy other people seemed to enjoy.

The array of gadgets, the mirrorless cameras, and the high-end computer were all parts of my pursuit to live the experiences that seemed so alluring when lived by others. The realization came slowly, pushing me to recalibrate my choices, to focus more on living within my means rather than getting entangled in the web of debts and repayments.

Reflecting on my journey from 18 to 27, it feels like a journey through a plethora of experiences and influences. The early years were about dazzle, fitting in, and acquiring to be recognized. However, as time progressed, the focus shifted from mere possessions to valuing experiences, and relishing the diverse flavors life presents.

Today, my dance with consumerism is more balanced, more attuned to my needs, my capacities. The allure is still there, the echoes of "spend, spend" still resonate, but my steps are more measured, my choices more reflective of my true desires rather than the fleeting influences around me. The journey is still on, the dance still continues, but now it's more harmonious, more in sync with the music of my heart.

In this relentless pursuit of consumerism, fueled by social pressures, every one of us has had our dance with debt, our entanglement with desires. The echoes of our past spending linger, reminding us of the choices made and the lessons learned. It's a journey, a continuous dance between desire and reality, between possession and fulfillment. And through the dance, we learn, we grow, and we find our rhythm, our melody in the intricate symphony of life with money.

Marketing tactics that promote overspending

Marketing is powerful—it's no secret. It shapes our desires, nudges our subconscious, and triggers impulses we never knew existed. In a world brimming with vibrant visuals and ceaseless advertisements, understanding the mechanisms that drive us to overspend is crucial. Here, we will delve deep into the various marketing strategies that encourage overspending, hoping to shed light on their impact on consumer behavior and the ever-lurking urge to spend.

Marketing tactics that promote overspending are pervasive, subtly penetrating our decision-making processes, making them incredibly effective. Among these are scarcity and urgency, stimulating a fear of missing out (FOMO) and generating an impulsive response to procure items before they run out. Social proof and peer pressure operate on our inherent need for social validation, propelling us towards purchases influenced by others' preferences and endorsements. The act of upselling and cross-selling is masterfully executed, urging customers to spend more under the guise of value addition. The provision of credit and financing options facilitates acquisitions we can't immediately afford, leading us into a labyrinth of debts and financial commitments. Reward programs and loyalty points give an illusion of gaining while spending, ensuring continual patronage. Lastly, the emotional appeal and branding connect us with brands on a deeper level, associating products with feelings, aspirations, and values.

I too have walked this labyrinthine journey of marketing intricacies. The tendrils of various marketing tactics have left imprints on my purchasing behaviors, compelling my younger self to fall into the cycle of overindulgence and impulsiveness. Today, I might be more conscious, more aware, but the lure still exists, simmering in the shadows, teasing the subconscious.

The concept of scarcity and urgency played me like a fiddle during my younger years, especially when it came to shoes. I remember the hours spent in line at Nice Kicks in San Francisco, hoping against hope to lay my hands on the latest limited-release shoes. Regardless of my financial position, the allure of owning these rare gems propelled me to spend, week after week, paycheck after paycheck. Many of these treasures, like Yeezy Turtle Doves and Supreme Jordan 5s, had to be sacrificed to the gods of debt, their sale aiding my financial recovery. The fervor even seeped into my relationship, as exemplified by the Yeezy Moonrocks acquisition, made on a special day—our one-year anniversary. It was the allure, the exclusivity that overshadowed everything else, leading to delays in our celebration.

Similarly, the "ONLY 3 left in stock" notification on websites has triggered an impulsive response in me on numerous occasions. The scarcity made me perceive the item as a hot commodity, compelling me to buy it instantaneously. Specifics might elude me, but the rush to acquire limited-drop gaming mice, amidst moving expenses, stands out, exemplifying the impulsive decisions spurred by scarcity.

As this urge for exclusivity persisted, it found its way into other aspects of my life, notably my tech gear. I vividly recall the day the Finalmouse Starlight-12 wireless gaming mouse was released. It was 2 pm, and I was shopping at IKEA, having just moved into my fiancé's place. With only a few minutes to spare before the launch, the air was thick with anticipation. I rallied everyone around me— my girlfriend and former roommates—to assist in this quest, our phones at the ready to snag this coveted piece of tech. As the clock struck the hour, amidst the IKEA aisles, a frantic purchasing spree ensued. In the end, only I managed to secure the mouse in my cart, despite being financially strapped due to the move. The limited availability of the mouse, combined with its rave reviews, overpowered my financial prudence. Now, whenever I glance at the mouse, it's not just a device; it's a reminder of my impulsive decisions driven by rarity.

The omnipresence of influencers on social media platforms has shaped my buying preferences and exposed me to products I never knew I needed. Their engaging content and credibility in my eyes made their endorsements effective, making me seek products that aligned with my needs and interests. These platforms made me believe in the utility and desirability of products, ensuring that I only sought those that promised value or improvement in my life.

Rewards programs and their tantalizing offers have been my constant companions. My penchant for boba teas during college was fueled by the stamp-collecting spree, each stamp bringing me closer to a free drink. The poke place cards I carry even now remind me of the continued allure of rewards, a subtle nudge towards loyalty and repeated patronage.

The array of marketing tactics is expansive, impacting us in multifaceted ways. Upselling and cross-selling paint a picture of value addition, presenting bundles and premium options as irresistible offers, steering us towards spending more. Credit and financing options act as enablers, allowing us to venture beyond our means and embrace a lifestyle fueled by debts and repayments. Meanwhile, emotional appeal and branding forge connections, making us perceive products as embodiments of our aspirations and values, adding a layer of desirability to the acquisition.

It's evident that these marketing tactics, designed with precision and understanding of human psychology, have an extensive impact. They create a whirlpool of emotions, decisions, and actions, influencing not just our buying preferences but also our perceptions of value and need. The layers of influence are intricate, blending the allure of rewards, the desire for social validation, and the fear of missing out, creating a concoction that makes overspending seem justified, if not desirable.

Each strategy leverages a different aspect of human behavior, creating scenarios where our rationality is overshadowed by impulses and desires. The influence is subtle yet profound, operating not just on our conscious minds but also on our subconscious, molding our perceptions, and guiding our actions. The dance with marketing is intricate, and the music is enchanting, but understanding the steps and recognizing the tunes can empower us to navigate the floor with awareness and control.

Remember, the journey of deciphering marketing tactics is continuous. The interplay of various strategies and their impact on our decision-making processes evolve with time and experience. Staying vigilant and informed is our shield against the relentless waves of marketing persuasion. The allure might be ever-present, the temptations might be continual, but the understanding and acknowledgment of their influence are our first steps towards mindful consumption and financial well-being.

The illusion of affordability

The illusion of affordability is a compelling phenomenon, a siren call that often leads many down the slippery slope of financial instability. It is underpinned by the subtle allure of seemingly manageable expenses, easy financing options, and the charm of minimal monthly payments, creating a façade of financial ease. This illusion often masks the long-term ramifications, the accumulated impact of deferred payments and accruing interests, creating a labyrinth of financial obligations. The tantalizing promise of immediate gratification often overshadows the consequential financial burden, fueling a cycle of overindulgence and financial strain.

This illusion manifests in various forms, ranging from the transient thrill of sales to the deceptive allure of financing options, enveloping consumers in a bubble of false economic security. The concept of "Buy Now, Pay Later," coupled with the enticing appeal of sales and discounts, plays into the psychological predisposition for immediate rewards, fostering a culture of impulsive buying and deferred financial responsibility. The impact of this illusion is profound, subtly altering spending habits, fostering a perpetual sense of economic pressure, and engendering a relentless pursuit of transient material joys.

In my journey through the tempting waters of consumerism, I too have danced with the illusion of affordability, particularly through financing options like PayPal Credit. This service transformed my approach to online purchases over $100, promising a sanctuary from interest as long as the balance was settled in six months. It was this illusion of manageable payments that propelled me to procure my $1.4k PC and reserve flights and hotels exceeding $3k. The subsequent struggle to allocate funds each month was a constant companion, occasionally slipping my mind, nudging me to make adjustments elsewhere. A vivid example is my current conundrum—a $3k hotel bill for my bachelor party looming over my head, with only two months left before a wave of six months' worth of interest hits me. While I received contributions from friends, the necessity to clear other debts led me to redirect these funds, leaving me scrambling to settle the impending PayPal debt.

However, my experiences with minimum payments are a different ballgame. The essence of my financial approach is a relentless pursuit to clear debts promptly, sometimes leading me to tighten my belt significantly. There were times I found solace in minimalistic meals of ramen and eggs, skipping others to steer clear of the interest trap. Despite my best efforts, my zeal occasionally outpaced my financial capacity, landing me in situations where paying off debts all at once was a battle, causing me to begrudgingly part with hundreds in interest.

The frenzied allure of Black Friday is another battleground. The anticipation and the subsequent rush to procure items on my wishlist, often propelled by savings from November, are familiar rituals. My love for new acquisitions, be it the latest GoPro, camera gear, or video games, found an outlet during these sales. Yet, I've noticed a deceptive practice wherein some sales aren't genuinely cheaper. I've seen items increase in price only to be "discounted," making the sale price nearly identical to the original. This tactic, though creating an illusion of a deal, is merely an enticing facade to prompt purchases. However, the ensuing dance with consumer debt was a stark reminder of the transient joys, often consuming any funds received during Christmas or my December birthday. There were times, like last year, where my financial entanglements forced a semblance of restraint, limiting my acquisitions to mere socks.

Surprisingly, small daily expenses never really enticed me into their deceptive dance. My focus remained tethered to specific desires and immediate gratifications rather than accumulating daily indulgences. My financial adventures were more about the immediate thrill of acquisitions rather than the subtle drain of daily expenses.

The illusion of affordability is a multifaceted entity, interweaving various elements to create a tapestry of deceptive allure. From financing options to minimal payments, from the frenzy of Black Friday to the charm of daily indulgences, every aspect contributes to the overall illusion. The experiences narrated illustrate the extensive influence of this illusion, shaping financial decisions, altering lifestyles, and inducing a sense of economic pressure. The subtle dynamics between immediate gratification and deferred financial responsibility underscore the profound impact of this illusion on consumer behavior and financial stability. The journey through this labyrinth of illusions is a constant learning curve, a continuous exploration of balancing desires with financial prudence, and a relentless pursuit of true economic freedom.

Predatory lending practices

Predatory lending practices are the bane of consumer financial health. They are exploitative tactics lenders employ to trap unsuspecting borrowers into unfavorable loan terms, leading to financial ruin, perpetual debt, and, often, insurmountable mental anguish. It is crucial to dissect these manipulative and damaging practices to equip individuals with the knowledge to avoid these treacherous financial pitfalls.

1. High-Interest Payday Loans

Payday loans, usually sought due to immediate financial needs, are notorious for their exorbitant interest rates. Lenders, capitalizing on the borrower's desperation, often do not fully disclose the true nature of these rates and the subsequent repayment expectations. These loans are characterized by short repayment terms and compound interest, making them one of the most costly loan options available. The relentless cycle of borrowing and the accumulation of interest often lead borrowers to financial ruin, with the owed amount swiftly exceeding the original borrowed sum.

Imagine this scenario:
1. You find yourself short on cash to cover an unexpected expense, like a car repair. Needing the money immediately, you decide to take out a $500 payday loan, intending to repay it by your next paycheck.
2. However, if you're unable to pay it back within the stipulated short-term (often two weeks), the loan's interest kicks in. Given the staggering average annual interest rate of 400% associated with payday loans, your debt starts to grow rapidly.
3. After just a few weeks, instead of owing the initial $500, you might find yourself in debt for well over $2,000 due to the crippling interest and fees
4. To manage this mounting debt, you might feel compelled to take out additional loans, beginning a vicious cycle. Each new loan adds to the debt, straining your budget and pushing you further into financial turmoil.

2. Auto-Loan Misrepresentation

Auto-loan misrepresentation is another common predatory lending practice. Borrowers are often drawn in by seemingly manageable loan terms, only to later discover undisclosed fees and skyrocketing interest rates. Hidden clauses and the fine print can turn what initially seemed like an affordable investment into a burdensome financial commitment. This not only strains a borrower's finances but can also mislead them into thinking they're getting a better deal than they actually are.

Imagine this scenario:

1. You decide it's time to buy your first car. After some browsing, you find the perfect one that fits your budget and needs.
2. The dealer offers an auto loan with seemingly attractive terms. They present a monthly payment of $700, which seems a little higher for your budget, but they said they can work with you.
3. Wanting to lower your monthly payments even more, the dealer suggests extending the loan term. Instead of a 48-month loan, they propose a 72-month loan. The monthly payments now drop to $250. On the surface, it feels like a win, and you sign the agreement.
4. Soon after, you discover hidden fees and an interest rate that's much higher than you were led to believe. Though your monthly payments are $250, due to these hidden costs, you're actually paying more in the long run.
5. The extended loan term means you're accumulating more interest over time, inflating the overall cost of the car. Additionally, cars depreciate quickly. If you were to try and sell the car in a few years, its value would be less than what you owe on the loan, leaving you in a financial quagmire.

3. Mortgage Traps

Mortgage traps, often associated with adjustable-rate mortgages, beguile borrowers with low initial interest rates. However, once the introductory period concludes, interest rates balloon, causing monthly payments to skyrocket unpredictably. This sudden and unexpected surge in financial commitment can lead to overwhelming stress and, in severe cases, foreclosure, leaving families displaced and financially drained.

Imagine this sequence of events:
1. You're hunting for a house, and after an exhaustive search, you finally stumble upon your dream home.
2. The bank offers an adjustable-rate mortgage that seems perfect. The initial rate is a mere 3%, resulting in affordable monthly payments that fit comfortably within your budget.
3. Delighted by the seemingly low cost, you sign the mortgage papers, believing you've secured a great deal.
4. A few years roll by smoothly, but then, without much warning, your interest rate adjusts drastically. It jumps from the initial 3% to a staggering 9%.
5. This rate hike pushes your monthly mortgage payment from a manageable $1,200 to an overwhelming $2,300. Annually, that's an unplanned increase of $13,200.
6. The heightened cost starts to eat into your savings. You find yourself reallocating money meant for other essentials like healthcare, children's education, or even basic living expenses. The dream home now feels more like a financial albatross, threatening your stability and peace of mind.

4. Credit Card Debts

Credit cards, while useful financial tools, can become instruments of economic destruction when coupled with predatory lending practices. Multiple credit card offers bombard consumers, each promising a plethora of benefits and seemingly manageable interest rates. However, when entangled in numerous card debts, the challenge begins. High interest, late payment penalties, and varied fees make the repayment process daunting and intricate. Balancing several cards, managing due dates, and mitigating the accumulating interest becomes a consuming, daily endeavor.

Imagine this sequence:
1. You receive a slew of credit card offers, each more appealing than the last, promising rewards, cashbacks, and low-interest rates.

2. Enticed by these offers, you sign up for multiple cards, thinking you can manage and benefit from the rewards.
3. Over time, you rack up a total balance of $5,000 across these cards, believing you'll pay it off steadily.
4. However, with average interest rates hovering around 16%, without any additional spending, your total debt grows to $5,800 in just one year due to interest accumulation alone.
5. As you juggle various due dates and try to keep up with minimum payments, you occasionally miss a few, incurring late payment fees.
6. With the added fees and continued interest, your original $5,000 debt feels insurmountable. The monthly payments barely scratch the surface, and the principal amount seems unyielding.

The human cost of predatory lending is profound, extending beyond mere financial implications. The victims of these unscrupulous practices often experience severe emotional and psychological stress, living under the constant shadow of debt. The relentless pursuit of repayment can lead to anxiety, depression, and a pervasive sense of hopelessness, exacerbating the overall impact of such lending practices on individual lives and well-being.

Predatory lenders prey on the most vulnerable and financially uninformed sectors of the population. Those with limited financial literacy, low income, or poor credit histories are the most susceptible to such manipulative tactics. The lenders exploit the desperation and lack of knowledge, ensuring that the borrowers are ensnared in unfavorable loan terms, escalating the cycle of debt and financial instability.

Addressing predatory lending practices necessitates robust legislative efforts and consumer protection policies. Regulatory bodies and governments must enforce strict guidelines to ensure full disclosure of loan terms, fees, and interest rates. Consumer awareness programs are pivotal to educate individuals about their rights, the nature of predatory lending, and the signs of exploitative loan terms. Empowering consumers with knowledge and legal protection is instrumental in combating predatory lending practices and fostering a fair lending environment.

The ramifications of predatory lending extend to the broader economic ecosystem. The perpetual cycle of debt and financial instability hampers economic growth by limiting consumer spending and savings. It undermines financial institutions' integrity and fosters an environment of distrust and apprehension towards lending practices. The collective economic strain induced by predatory lending practices necessitates a reevaluation of lending norms and the implementation of equitable lending policies.

Predatory lending practices are multifaceted financial traps that exploit consumer vulnerability, lack of information, and immediate financial needs. They manifest across various lending sectors, each characterized by deceptive presentations, concealed fees, and oppressive interest rates. The implications are profound, affecting individual financial stability, mental well-being, and the broader economic landscape.

To mitigate the impact of such practices, comprehensive legislative efforts, consumer protection policies, and financial education are imperative. A proactive approach to understanding, identifying, and combating predatory lending is the cornerstone to fostering financial health, consumer trust, and equitable economic development. The fight against predatory lending is not just a financial battle; it is a moral and ethical imperative to protect the most vulnerable from economic exploitation and psychological distress.

Credit Score System

The credit score system, a seemingly innocuous numerical representation of financial reliability, has become a cornerstone of modern financial identity. It's a ubiquitous metric, influencing numerous financial decisions, from loan approvals to interest rates, shaping individual financial landscapes and dictating financial trajectories. It's a system steeped in paradox, offering opportunities while potentially leading to financial entrapment.

The concept of a credit score has been ingrained in my financial consciousness since my formative years, a lesson imparted by my grandmother who emphasized its paramount importance. While the value of a good credit score is undeniable, the pursuit of it, I've realized, can be a precarious journey, potentially leading to a quagmire of debt. The delicate dance between utilizing and repaying debt to build credit is a double-edged sword, opening doors to financial opportunities but also to potential pitfalls.

My initial foray into the world of credit was during high school, a journey overseen by my grandmother, ensuring responsible usage. However, as I transitioned into college and subsequently into adulthood, the allure of a more affluent lifestyle, enriched experiences, and superior possessions became irresistible. Despite my resolve to repay all debts promptly and in full, the cycle of using future earnings for current debts became a relentless rhythm, a cycle that seemed to be in perpetual motion, with every paycheck earmarked for debts incurred.

This cycle, while seemingly boosting my credit score to an impressive 760, left me with a lingering sense of regret for not prioritizing savings. It seems there's a generational divide in financial priorities, with the older generation venerating the credit score, while the younger demographic seems to value savings and investments more. The decision to finance purchases like my car and my engagement ring, despite having the funds, was made with the intention of building credit and maintaining an emergency fund. However, this strategy backfired, leading to the depletion of my savings and reliance on future earnings.

Reflecting on this journey, I can't help but ponder the paradoxical nature of the credit score system. It's a silent puppeteer, pulling the strings, dictating our financial decisions, and subtly influencing our relationship with money and debt. It's a system that, while ostensibly offering financial empowerment, can inadvertently lead to financial entrapment, a scenario I've experienced firsthand.

The pursuit of a stellar credit score, while seemingly prudent, made me overlook the essence of financial stability—savings and investments. It's a realization that dawned upon me as I navigated the intricate labyrinth of credit and debt, a journey marked by silent battles, unspoken regrets, and lessons learned. The allure of credit, the promise of financial growth, and the pursuit of a numerical representation of my financial reliability became a dance with shadows, a dance that, in hindsight, I wish had been more balanced, more attuned to the silent tunes of financial prudence and foresight.

The credit score system, with its pervasive influence and omnipresence, serves as a constant reminder of the intricate interplay between financial empowerment and entrapment. It's a system that necessitates a delicate balance, a nuanced understanding, and a mindful approach to financial decisions, ensuring that the pursuit of a favorable score doesn't compromise the foundational pillars of financial stability and well-being.

In the age of instant gratification and endless opportunities, modern debt has evolved into a complex entity that permeates every aspect of our financial lives. From the tempting simplicity of "buy now, pay later" schemes to the intricate web of the credit score system, every choice presents its unique set of challenges. Our consumerist culture, amplified by relentless marketing strategies, consistently tugs at our financial heartstrings, pushing us towards purchases that promise belonging and status. Yet, behind these shiny facades lie the deceptive traps of affordability illusions and the ominous shadows of predatory lending. The promise of easy financing and the societal pressure to conform mask the lurking dangers, often leading to a vortex of debt and financial instability. Equally, the ubiquitous credit score, while framing our financial reliability, can become a double-edged sword—opening doors or barring them shut. Navigating this complex landscape requires awareness, diligence, and often, a resistance to the overwhelming currents of consumerism. Understanding modern debt is not just about numbers or interest rates; it's about recognizing the forces that drive us, the choices we make, and the consequences we must inevitably bear.

THE PSYCHOLOGY BEHIND BORROWING

The instant gratification vs. long-term pain

In a society dominated by consumerism and a plethora of choices, the constant struggle between succumbing to instant gratification and experiencing long-term pain is palpable. This struggle is particularly evident in the realm of personal finance, where the accessibility of credit and the ease of making purchases can lead to significant financial strain and regret. The allure of immediate pleasure can often overshadow the potential long-term consequences, creating a cycle of spending and debt that is difficult to escape. This battle between the present self, who yearns for immediate satisfaction, and the future self, who bears the burden of consequences, is deeply embedded in the psychology of borrowing and spending.

Many individuals experience the tension between the desire to satisfy immediate needs or wants and the realization of the enduring repercussions of their financial decisions. The accessibility of credit cards and online shopping platforms has amplified this struggle, creating opportunities for impulsive purchases and facilitating a lifestyle that might not be sustainable in the long run. The ease and convenience these mediums provide enable a pattern of spending that is often only examined when the long-term pain becomes evident.

In my own experiences, I've certainly been no stranger to the allure of impulsive purchases. This instant gratification, particularly revolving around food and dining, has often landed me in financial strains. Opting for a higher-end steak or an additional appetizer because it sounded appealing at the moment, or frequently ordering from delivery apps like GrubHub, Postmates, and Uber Eats due to laziness to cook, exemplified my lack of foresight. These instances of immediate pleasure, though seemingly inconsequential at the time, resulted in significant regret. I found myself contemplating the substantial amount of money I could have saved and allocated towards more pertinent needs like student loans.

Similarly, accompanying my fiancée during her shopping excursions led to moments of impulsive buying. While she shopped, I'd meander around the mall and find myself attracted to items that I didn't necessarily need. I recall a time I bought a starter pack of One Piece Trading Card Game cards simply to kill time, only for them to collect dust for months. I didn't even play the game, nor did I have the time or friends to play with. It was a fleeting desire to experience the pleasure of acquiring something new that led to such unplanned and unnecessary purchases.

Moreover, it wasn't just the large, noticeable expenses that added to the financial burden; the small, seemingly insignificant ones played a pivotal role too. Occasional dinners, fuel expenses, trinkets, and books accumulated stealthily. When the credit card statement finally arrived, the sheer amount from these small, varied expenses was startling. The cycle of buying on credit, exhausting the paycheck to clear debts, and then reverting to credit for necessities was relentless and consuming.

Such a routine indeed builds a façade of transient euphoria, yet the impending financial stress is formidable. I constantly found myself choosing the ephemeral greatness, fully aware of the impending bat strike. However, with increased financial literacy and awareness, I've significantly reduced my reliance on credit cards and impulsive buying. The technique of adding items to the cart to experience the thrill of shopping, imagining the satisfaction, and then not checking out has proven to be a successful strategy in battling these urges.

The psychological dynamics between immediate gratification and enduring pain are complex. Instant gratification can offer a temporary escape from reality, a momentary taste of joy and fulfillment. However, this transient happiness is often followed by a prolonged period of regret, financial strain, and stress. The realization of the repercussions of impulsive spending serves as a painful reminder of the importance of financial prudence and foresight.

The journey of learning and evolving from such experiences is crucial. By fostering a deeper understanding of personal finance, embracing financial literacy, and developing strategies to curb impulsive spending, individuals can navigate the turbulent waters of financial decision-making more effectively. Becoming conscious of the transient nature of immediate pleasures and cultivating a mindset focused on long-term well-being is instrumental in breaking the cycle of instant gratification and long-term pain, leading to a more balanced and harmonious financial life.

The link between self-worth and material possessions

The intertwining of self-worth and material possessions is a widespread phenomenon, deeply ingrained in many societies and cultures. Often, our consumerist environment nurtures the concept that possessing the latest and the most luxurious items directly correlates with our self-value and societal ranking. This prevailing connection can foster detrimental habits, potentially encouraging individuals to seek external validation and societal approval through acquisition, often neglecting the consequential financial and emotional turmoil that may ensue. Let's delve deep into this relationship between our sense of worth and the material possessions we accumulate, understand its roots, and contemplate its profound implications on our lives and well-being.

The perpetual cycle of equating self-worth to possessions can be subtly coercive. The incessant societal and peer pressures may push individuals to perpetually acquire, pushing them into a never-ending spiral of consumption. The desire to project an image of success and wealth drives purchasing decisions, often leading to financial stress and creating a paradox where the pursuit of worth becomes a pursuit of perpetual dissatisfaction and unfulfillment. It's crucial to comprehend the transient nature of material satisfaction and re-evaluate the true essence of self-worth, discerning it from the superficial gratification that possessions provide.

High school years are a formative time where the link between self-worth and material possessions became glaringly apparent to me. I remember persuading my grandmother to buy me a Yamaha Custom Z Alto Saxophone. This wasn't merely about playing music; it was a statement. I wanted to project an image of a serious player, someone who was committed and skillful, and owning the latest and most sophisticated saxophone seemed like the way to do it. This pricy instrument did help me win awards, but once I got to college, the charm started to fade. The college jazz band did not provide the same level of enthusiasm and fulfillment that I experienced in high school, leaving me contemplating the actual worth of my high-priced saxophone. This contemplation led me to understand that an intermediate-priced saxophone could have served the purpose just as well, highlighting how the desire for prestige shaped my decisions.

During college, the allure of name brand clothing entangled me in its web, where the notion of being valued by my peers was closely linked to the brand tags on my clothes. Levi jeans, Nike, Adidas, clothing from Nordstrom and Neiman Marcus became symbols of my societal value. These pieces, which were ostensibly 'in trend,' were not even my style, and I didn't wear them after a while. Despite this, I indulged in this expensive pursuit, trying to fit in and be as "classy" as my friends who flaunted their designer gear. The temporary satisfaction these items provided contrasted sharply with their lasting financial implications, a realization that made me grateful for my financial constraints during that time.

The illusion of increased self-worth that came with acquiring material possessions was invariably short-lived. People would glance, admire momentarily, and then move on, leaving me with a closet full of expensive items and a lingering sense of unfulfillment. My fascination with shoes in college is a testament to this fleeting satisfaction. The investment in hot release shoes, which didn't even suit my style, reflected my struggle for acceptance and validation. Eventually, the burden of credit card bills overshadowed the transient joy of possessing Air Jordans, forcing me to revert to my comfortable skater shoes and confront the financial repercussions of my purchases.

The superficiality of material possessions became evident, revealing a harsh reality: the pursuit of external validation through possessions is a hollow endeavor. People generally don't care about what you have, and if they do, they are likely grappling with the same internal battle. Reflecting on my younger years, the role of materialistic values in my financial well-being became increasingly clear. The expensive shoes and clothes bought on credit cards only served to deepen my financial woes and heightened my understanding of the futility of seeking worth through material acquisition.

Material possessions, as a metric of self-worth, are transient and invariably lead to a cycle of dissatisfaction. The fleeting admiration and the temporary sense of achievement do not outweigh the lingering feelings of emptiness and the financial strain that often accompanies excessive consumption. Our environment, rich with consumerism and external validations, consistently nudges us towards equating our value with our possessions, making it imperative to cultivate self-awareness and discernment.

Recognizing the transient nature of material gratification, it's crucial to detach our sense of worth from external possessions and redefine the essence of self-value. This involves a deep and intentional reflection on our true needs, values, and aspirations, going beyond the ephemeral allure of materialism. A genuine sense of self-worth stems from internal attributes, personal achievements, moral values, and the quality of our relationships, rather than the transient satisfaction derived from material possessions.

Understanding and acknowledging the inherent value within ourselves and dissociating it from the material possessions we acquire is a step towards fostering healthier self-perception and emotional well-being. It involves looking beyond the societal norms and pressures and cultivating an intrinsic sense of self-worth, grounded in our true selves rather than external validations. By doing so, we can break free from the relentless cycle of consumption and attain a more profound, lasting sense of fulfillment and contentment. The journey might be challenging, filled with introspection and unlearning, but it's a necessary pursuit for those seeking to find true worth beyond the material world.

Fear of missing out (FOMO)

In an era characterized by ceaseless connectivity and the continual flow of shared experiences, the Fear of Missing Out—commonly known as FOMO—is an increasingly prevalent psychological phenomenon. FOMO fuels a pervasive anxiety, an unease arising from the possibility of missed opportunities, unattended events, or unexplored destinations. This condition is not merely a whimsical concept; it is a catalyst for decisions, behaviors, and, more profoundly, a progenitor of financial stresses. The essence of FOMO lies in the pursuit of shared experiences and social validation, often leading individuals to prioritize the immediate pleasures of participation over the long-term ramifications of financial imprudence.

While the notion of FOMO predominantly resonates with experiences and social events, its implications extend into the realms of financial stability and fiscal responsibility. The struggle between the desire to be part of every social gathering, every memory, every shared laughter, and the financial constraints that reality imposes creates a turbulent dichotomy. This dichotomy oftentimes culminates in financial decisions that prioritize immediate social gratification over long-term financial wellbeing.

Our inherent longing for experiences that resonate and moments that define our narratives has steered many, including myself, into the intricate web of FOMO. My tryst with this phenomenon has mostly revolved around experiences, instances where the magnetic allure of an opportunity overwhelmed my financial discretion. One poignant example of this was a winery trip to Napa, California. The call of fine wine, the elegant ambience, and the shared laughter seemed like a rendezvous with luxury—a luxury that translated into debt and financial stress. While the trip was a cornucopia of cherished moments, the subsequent paycheck became a vessel to offset the debt incurred, underscoring the unrelenting compromise between experiences and financial stability.

The pull of FOMO became overwhelmingly powerful when I received an invitation to a close friend's engagement party in the breathtaking islands of Fiji. The mere thought of missing out on such a significant event was unbearable, especially considering the rarity of such occasions. My elation knew no bounds; being invited to such a momentous celebration was a true honor. However, beneath this ecstatic anticipation lay the undeniable reality—I didn't have the funds for such a lavish trip.

Yet, the prospect of experiencing Fiji authentically, given that my friend's family hailed from there, with some still residing in this paradise, was too tempting. This wasn't just any touristy adventure; we were treated to genuine local experiences. We savored local delicacies, visited the renowned Hindu temple in Nadi town near

Denarau, danced vibrantly to Indian tunes during the festivities, and hopped across islands, absorbing Fiji's raw beauty. An unforgettable highlight for me was chartering a boat, complete with a captain, to chase waves of Fiji. Not to brag, but I surfed Cloud Break. Every moment was worth its weight in gold.

However, this trip, as magical as it was, came with its set of financial challenges. The total expenses soared to an eye-watering $6,000, which I managed by plunging into debt, leaning heavily on my credit card. In the months that followed, my heart fluttered with the cherished memories of the trip, while simultaneously grappling with the hefty financial aftermath. It's a testament to the complex dynamics of FOMO—where the profound joy of treasured memories can, at times, overshadow sound financial judgment. Even so, I remain profoundly grateful for the experience and the opportunity to be part of such a joyous occasion, even if it meant compromising my financial stability temporarily.

Living in a city vibrant with social avenues like San Francisco augments the struggles with FOMO. The city pulsates with so many events, gatherings, and social rendezvous, each beckoning with the promise of shared memories and collective experiences. This constant enticement often leads to a perpetual cycle of social participation and financial expenditure. The struggle with FOMO becomes a continual quest to balance social inclinations with financial realities, to tread the fine line between collective experiences and individual financial solace.

Managing FOMO is akin to walking a tightrope—a precarious balance between desires and realities. Living in California while my family resides in Texas adds another layer of complexity. The geographical distance translates into costly travel expenses, especially during peak seasons like the holidays. The financial weight of traveling becomes even more pronounced during such times. For instance, I had to forgo Thanksgiving with them to ensure that I could be there for Christmas, trying to optimize both emotional and financial considerations. Moreover, when monumental family events like graduations or significant celebrations arise, I'm faced with the decision of churning out money for a plane ticket, taking vacation days, and dealing with the associated expenses, whether I have the funds at hand or not. Embracing financial transparency and fostering open conversations about my financial limitations have been pivotal in this journey. The quest to maintain connections and nurture relationships often leads to financial compromises, especially when these moments are family-centric. It becomes a profound dilemma, forcing me to weigh the significance of familial bonds against the financial repercussions. This continuous negotiation between wanting to be present at every family function and grappling with the associated costs underscores the intricate interplay between emotional connections and financial constraints.

While my experiences with FOMO have largely been detached from the influences of social media, the role of these platforms in amplifying this phenomenon cannot be understated. Social media serves as a relentless mirror, reflecting a montage of extravagant trips, lavish lifestyles, and seamless happiness. For many, these virtual windows cultivate envy, inflate inadequacies, and accentuate the fear of missing out on perceived paradises. The constant bombardment of seemingly perfect lives can exacerbate feelings of FOMO, pushing individuals to pursue similar experiences, often with disregard to their financial capabilities.

The symbiosis between social media and FOMO is intricate; one amplifies the appeal of the other. When acquaintances embark on luxurious voyages or indulge in opulent experiences, the visual journey they share ignites a latent desire to experience similar extravagances, fueling the cycle of comparison and dissatisfaction. Even for those like me, who prefer to traverse international terrains on their terms, the magnetism of shared experiences on social platforms can invoke subtle envy, sparking contemplation over missed opportunities and unexplored terrains.

The endeavor to manage FOMO is a continual struggle—a relentless battle between the yearning to be part of every memory and the pragmatic realization of financial constraints. For some, this struggle is a convoluted journey marked by introspection, restraint, and an evolving understanding of one's needs and desires. The multifaceted nature of FOMO makes its management a complex task, intertwined with emotional intricacies, social expectations, and individual aspirations. It's a journey of learning to say no, of understanding one's limits, and of redefining one's perspective on what truly matters.

FOMO, deeply embedded in our social fabric, exerts a powerful influence over our choices and experiences. Its impact is not just limited to social engagement; it extends to financial stability and emotional health. As we journey through life, there will be moments where we must reckon with and manage our FOMO. Some experiences, despite the temporary financial strain they might impose, are truly priceless. For someone like me, who didn't have the funds at the time, opting for debt was my chosen path. Yet, for another who has prepared financially, the decision might come without any financial stress. It's all about choices and determining what's truly valuable to us. Navigating this complex landscape requires introspection, awareness, and a consistent effort to weigh immediate joys against lasting implications. Amidst the dilemmas and challenges, the quest for a balanced life, devoid of relentless fear and constant comparisons, is a noble endeavor.

Debt as a way to bridge the gap between desires and reality.

The leverage that debt provides is a double-edged sword; it enables the realization of dreams, acquisitions, and experiences, but it also imposes a lingering obligation—a commitment to repay, often with the added burden of interest. This inevitable interaction between desires and tangible realities fosters a dynamic environment, where individuals often find themselves oscillating between the fulfillment of their wants and the subsequent obligation to amend their financial commitments. The ongoing dance between aspirations and reality necessitates mindful deliberation and thoughtful reflection on the true essence of needs and wants.

My journey with debt has been a tapestry of interactions, a complex interplay between my desires, my experiential aspirations, and my financial realities. I've navigated through situations where the temptation of experiences or possessions has obscured the underlying financial implications, leading to a careful reassessment of my financial bearings. A distinctive instance that stands out is my endeavor to be a part of every experiential opportunity, a consequence of my struggle with FOMO. The captivating charm of a friend's engagement in Fiji, for example, was a rendezvous with pristine beaches and vibrant cultures. Yet, it was also a financial undertaking, a $6,000 expedition that demanded a thoughtful financial reassessment in the subsequent months.

Similarly, the pursuit of my musical aspirations intertwined with my interaction with debt. The acquisition of a Yamaha Custom Z

Alto Saxophone during my high school years was not just an emblem of my musical commitment but also a manifestation of my desire to attain immediate recognition and acceptance. This acquisition, while financed by my grandmother, reflected my inclination to secure an instrument that would resonate with my peers and validate my musical prowess. This experience underscored the intricate relationship between my aspirations, my perceived self-worth, and my financial realities, highlighting the complex dynamics between desires and tangible limitations.

The interactions with debt extended to my sartorial preferences as well. During my college years, my inclination towards name brands was a reflection of my desire for social validation and acceptance. The acquisition of apparel from renowned brands like Levi, Nike, and Adidas wasn't just about style; it was about projecting an image, a manifestation of my social standing. This pursuit of high-end apparel, however, came at a considerable financial cost, highlighting the perpetual tension between my desire for social acceptance and the resulting financial implications.

The alignment of my sartorial preferences with my financial commitments was a journey marked by reflection and recalibration. The transition from high-end brands to more financially sustainable options wasn't just a shift in preferences; it was a conscious decision to align my expenditures with my financial capabilities. This evolution spotlighted the ongoing interplay between my aspirations, my yearning for social validation, and my financial obligations, illustrating how debt serves as a bridge between desires and tangible realities.

The intricate relationship between debt and desire is not isolated to specific experiences or acquisitions; it is a ubiquitous interaction that permeates various facets of life. The inclination to experience, to acquire, to be a part of something often clashes with the inherent financial limitations, necessitating the utilization of debt as a means to reconcile these contrasting entities. However, this interaction is not without its challenges; it demands a meticulous understanding of one's financial capacities and a thoughtful reflection on the implications of debt on long-term financial stability.

The utilization of debt as a bridge between desires and reality is a delicate dance, a constant interplay between aspirations and obligations. The chase of immediate gratification, the desire to be a part of something, and the pursuit of recognition often overshadow the underlying financial commitments, leading to a labyrinth of financial recalibrations and adjustments. Navigating through this labyrinth requires a conscious effort to align desires with realities, to prioritize needs over wants, and to understand the profound implications of debt on financial well-being.

Debt, as a financial tool, holds profound implications on an individual's life. It can be both an enabler, allowing for the realization of dreams and aspirations, and a tether, imposing lingering obligations and financial stresses. My experiences have provided me with profound insights into the intricate dynamics between debt, desires, and reality. The journey through various financial decisions, be it related to experiences, possessions, or self-validation, has underscored the importance of mindful deliberation and thoughtful reflection on the implications of debt.

In conclusion, the dance between debt, desires, and reality is a journey marked by continual learning, evolving understandings, and meticulous adjustments. The pursuit of dreams, experiences, and recognition, while facilitated by debt, necessitates a profound understanding of one's financial capabilities and a commitment to aligning aspirations with tangible realities. The journey is fraught with challenges, dilemmas, and reflections, but it is a journey that fosters growth, understanding, and a deeper appreciation for the delicate balance between desires and obligations. The dance continues, with each step echoing the intricate symphony of aspirations, realities, and the perpetual quest for financial harmony.

The emotional comfort of "fitting in"

The concept of "fitting in" is deeply ingrained in the human psyche, resonating with our inherent desire for social acceptance and communal harmony. This inclination to conform to societal norms, values, and expectations emerges from our innate need for social interactions, a fundamental aspect of human existence that has evolved over centuries. The comfort derived from fitting in is profound—it provides a sense of belonging, a feeling of security, and a validation of one's existence within a social framework. However, the pursuit of conformity can often lead to a compromise of one's individuality, a surrendering of personal values and beliefs to the collective consciousness.

The desire to fit in extends beyond simple social dynamics; it serves as an emotional refuge, a sanctuary for those yearning for communal acceptance. This craving for alignment with societal norms is an intricate interplay of emotions, reflections, and adjustments. It's a delicate balance between preserving one's individuality and blending into the social fabric, a dance that demands thoughtful deliberation, keen awareness, and often, emotional fortitude. The pursuit of this emotional harmony can pave the way for self-discovery, growth, and a profound comprehension of one's role within the societal mosaic.

The journey to fitting in has been an intricate part of my life, a labyrinth of emotions, reflections, and realizations. During my college years, this quest for social acceptance was particularly poignant, marked by a continuous oscillation between my inherent desires and societal expectations. I felt an intense need to align my preferences, my actions, and my lifestyle with what was deemed acceptable, with what would grant me the coveted badge of belonging. The pursuit of high-end apparel, the alignment with popular trends, and the adoption of prevalent lifestyles were all manifestations of this intrinsic desire to fit in, to be accepted, to be a part of something.

The emotional comfort derived from fitting in provided a sanctuary, a refuge from the solitude of individuality. It was a solace found in the harmonious synchronization with societal rhythms, a solace that, at times, overshadowed my inherent beliefs, my true preferences, and my authentic self. However, as the journey unfolded, as the dance between conformity and individuality continued, a transformation occurred. The realization that fitting in was not the epitome of social existence, that individuality had its own charm, its own allure, started to dawn upon me.

This transformative journey reached a pivotal point after my engagement. The prospect of building a life with someone, of merging two worlds into one, brought forth a profound reflection on my values, my beliefs, and my financial commitments. The realization that my financial decisions, my engagements with debt, had implications not just on my life, but on our collective future, was a wake-up call. I started viewing money, debt, and financial commitments from a different perspective, a perspective marked by responsibility, prudence, and a consideration for our collective well-being.

The yearning for social acceptance and the pursuit of "fitting in" is a journey many undertake, yet it's essential to realize that sometimes, the cost of blending in can be the erasure of one's unique essence. For too long, I believed my well-being was anchored in this act of conforming. But the emotional strain of forsaking oneself to fit a mold is a heavy burden to bear.

The transition from seeking social acceptance to embracing individuality and responsibility was not just a shift in perspective; it was a metamorphosis, a rebirth of my true self. The emotional comfort of fitting in started to fade away, replaced by the comfort found in authenticity, in being true to oneself and one's values. I learned that fitting in was not a prerequisite for social harmony, that individuality and diversity were the true essences of societal existence. The pursuit of conformity ceased to be the focal point of my existence, giving way to a deeper understanding of myself, my values, and my place in the world.

The journey of fitting in is a perennial one, encompassing a spectrum of emotions, experiences, and transformations. It's a journey marked by the pursuit of acceptance, the quest for emotional comfort, and the eventual realization of one's individuality. The transformation from seeking to fit in to embracing one's true self is a profound one, leading to a richer, more authentic existence. It's a metamorphosis that goes beyond mere social interactions, delving into the realms of self-discovery, self-acceptance, and self-love.

In conclusion, the emotional comfort of "fitting in" is a concept that resonates with our inherent human nature, our fundamental desire for acceptance and belonging. However, the true essence of existence lies in the embrace of our individuality, our authenticity, and our inherent values. The journey from conformity to individuality is a transformative one, leading to a deeper, more meaningful understanding of oneself and the world around us. The dance between fitting in and being true to oneself is a delicate one, but it's a dance that leads to the symphony of authentic existence, echoing the harmonious tunes of diversity, acceptance, and unconditional love.

DEBT'S EMOTIONAL TOLL

Sleepless nights and chronic worry

The specter of debt casts a long, imposing shadow, one that extends far beyond the numerical figures and the monthly statements. The emotional toll of debt is profound, with its impacts rippling through the very core of our well-being. It infiltrates our thoughts, our feelings, and our daily interactions, creating a vortex of stress, worry, and anxiety. The constant presence of this financial burden can turn days into a ceaseless battle with worry and nights into a restless dance with anxiety. However, the emotional ramifications of debt aren't always restricted to sleepless nights; they manifest in various forms and intensities, engulfing the mind in a turbulent sea of thoughts, affecting the calmness of our days and the peace of our nights.

One of the subtle, yet persistent, impacts of debt is the chronic worry it embeds within our minds. This worry isn't just a fleeting concern; it's a relentless companion, shadowing our every move, our every thought. It's this chronic worry that can lead to a loss of productive time, consumed by the incessant musings about the financial burdens that loom large over our heads. It's a lingering presence, a constant whisper in our ears, a perpetual reminder of the financial constraints that bind us.

For me, the emotional ramifications of debt never really translated into sleepless nights, but rather into daydreams permeated with stress and a persistent loss of productive time, consumed by thoughts of my debt. Each day would often turn into a battle, a struggle to focus on the task at hand, with my mind persistently wandering to the financial constraints that ensnared me. It felt like a shadow, sometimes faint, sometimes overwhelmingly opaque, following me through the corridors of my daily life, whispering the murmurs of financial worry into my ears.

These daydreams were not just mere wanderings of the mind; they were vivid reminders of the financial burden I bore, filled with the echoes of unpaid bills and unmet financial obligations. The constant mental calculations, the relentless what-ifs, and the perpetual strategizing to navigate the financial maze were exhausting. They were draining the vibrancy from my days, overshadowing the joys with the clouds of worry. It felt like a relentless tug-of-war between the present and the future, between enjoying the moment and preparing for the unseen, between living and surviving.

The emotional toll was not just a personal battle; it had repercussions on my professional life as well. The constant worry, the continuous strategizing, impacted my focus, my productivity, and my interactions. It was a silent, invisible barrier between me and my potential, a barrier that seemed to grow with every passing day. This constant companion of worry and stress was not just a byproduct of financial constraints; it was a testament to the overwhelming impact of debt on our emotional well-being.

However, the journey through this emotional turbulence was also a journey of self-discovery, a journey of resilience. It taught me the importance of financial prudence, the value of planning, and the significance of responsibility. It was a harsh, unforgiving teacher, but it was a teacher nonetheless, guiding me through the labyrinth of financial prudence and emotional resilience. The lessons learned were not just about numbers and calculations; they were about values, priorities, and a deeper understanding of my own self.

Reflecting on this journey, the emotional toll of debt emerges not just as a series of stressors but as a comprehensive experience affecting various facets of life. The chronic worry, the relentless stress, and the continuous struggle with financial constraints are not just individual experiences; they are the echoes of a collective struggle, a shared journey through the realms of financial burdens and emotional turmoil. The silent whispers of worry, the invisible shadows of stress, are the common companions of those ensnared in the chains of debt, marking their days with the imprints of financial worry and their nights with the echoes of unpaid bills.

The emotional impact of debt is profound, with its ramifications extending far beyond the mere financial constraints. It's an experience, affecting our days, our nights, our interactions, and our very well-being. It's a journey through the valleys of worry, the mountains of stress, and the rivers of anxiety, leading to a deeper understanding of oneself, one's values, and one's priorities. The chronic worry, the sleepless nights, or the daydreams of stress are the manifestations of this emotional journey, a journey that, despite its hardships, can lead to growth, resilience, and a renewed sense of self.

Strain on relationships and family dynamics

The whisperings of debt weave silently but substantially through the fabric of relationships, stretching the threads to their limits, coloring the dynamics with the shades of financial stress and strain. This uninvited guest sits at the dinner tables, lurks in the corners of intimate conversations, and influences decisions and actions, sometimes overtly, sometimes subtly. The impact of debt on relationships can vary, reaching beyond the immediate financial implications to affect the emotional, psychological, and social aspects of our connections. It can introduce an undercurrent of tension, a silent discord, that shapes interactions, decisions, and the overall atmosphere within relationships, especially within the familial realm.

In my sojourn through the silent battles of debt, the experiences of concealed financial strife have been a constant shadow, subtly influencing every aspect of my relationships, especially with my fiancée and family. The bottle of financial distress I held within me was perennially being filled and emptied in a controlled fashion, embodying my internal struggles, the tinges of regret, and the lessons learned. The genesis of these struggles was intertwined with the actions and decisions related to money usage, which sometimes led to disagreements with my fiancée. These were not necessarily conflicts borne out of monetary constraints but repercussions of the priorities attached to our expenditures.

One particular moment of discord arose from a situation where our aspirations were halted by my unavailability of funds. It was a simple, seemingly inconsequential incident, but it unveiled the layers of financial implications and the necessity for prudent planning. The shadows of this financial unrest didn't destabilize our bond, thanks to our near-decade of companionship and mutual understanding, but it did introduce a nuanced layer of tension within our relationship, a silent whisper of financial stress echoing in our shared spaces.

The web of my familial dynamics was consistently intertwined with threads of financial hardships and challenges. Necessities were never a luxury, but the stability of having a roof above and food on the table, at times facilitated by food stamps, always made their presence felt. It was my grandmother, a symbol of financial wisdom and diligence, who infused in me the principles of financial responsibility and money management. Her teachings were the guiding stars amidst the storm of financial recklessness I witnessed and, unfortunately, initially embraced.

In stark contrast, my parents were the embodiments of financial irresponsibility. The vivid imageries of my mother's unending wardrobe acquisitions and my father's indulgence in smoking and gambling painted my childhood memories with brush strokes of financial instability and irresponsibility. The moments of their blatant disregard for time and commitments, coupled with the looming threats of house foreclosures, sketched a tableau of financial fragility and familial strains.

These engrained memories and lived experiences came to a head when my father, a figure associated with years of financial frivolity and unfulfilled promises, reached out to me for financial assistance of $500.00. This request disrupted my meticulously crafted budgeting structures and plunged me into a vortex of unexpected stress and uncharted emotional territories. It was a convergence of familial obligations and financial rationality, a meeting point of the echoes of past financial transgressions and the newfound resolutions of financial prudence.

This wasn't merely a transaction of $500; it was a transaction steeped in unfulfilled promises, unmet responsibilities, and unspoken tensions resonating within the silent interludes of our interactions. The ask wasn't isolated; it was an echo of past financial imprudence, a reflection of my father's journey through unbridled financial extravagance and the subsequent shadows of financial instability. It was also a mirror reflecting my journey through the realization of financial responsibilities and the cultivation of financial discipline, all under the watchful eyes and wise words of my grandmother.

Amidst these shadows and echoes, I found resilience, a balance between the obligations to support my family and the commitment to walk the path of financial freedom. The looming shadows of potential familial financial requests are a ticking time bomb in the background, a constant reminder of the unknown future stresses that may arise. It's an intricate dance of managing familial expectations, adhering to financial commitments, and maintaining a focus on the future I envision for myself. But a daunting question arises, almost haunting in its persistence: "Do I start factoring in my future, or do I surrender it for my parents who find themselves in a precarious financial situation?"

This question isn't abstract or theoretical; it is rooted in the very fabric of my reality. I can vividly recall the numerous instances when my mother subtly, and sometimes not so subtly, hinted that my brother and I would be their support in their old age. Perhaps, it's a cultural sentiment, deeply rooted in Nepalese traditions, where the torch of responsibility is passed onto the children to ensure the well-being of their aging parents. But as a first-generation American, I grapple with this cultural notion, questioning its place in my hybrid identity.

Our familial home, their primary asset, is valued at around $250K in 2023. But beyond that, there isn't much. If they find themselves unable to work, who bears the responsibility for their sustenance? Their food, bills, property taxes, insurance - the list goes on. How can I, in good conscience, leave them vulnerable, potentially condemning them to a life of hardship and want? Yet, the very thought of shouldering this monumental responsibility fills me with trepidation. Can my six-figure 9-5 job truly suffice? My earnings, once a source of personal comfort and security, now seem stretched thin as I ponder a future supporting multiple individuals. Their journey of raising my brother and me, with all its inherent challenges, looms over me as a template. How will I navigate a similar path, especially with the added financial pressures?

The weight of this contemplation is immense, and the ambiguity surrounding the future often keeps me up at night. But one thing is clear: I must forge a balance, a sustainable solution that respects both my responsibilities towards my parents and my aspirations for personal growth and stability. The road ahead is uncertain, but it's one I am determined to traverse, equipped with the lessons of the past and the hopes for the future." This struggle, this balancing act, is not just about the immediate financial implications; it's about navigating the intricate layers of familial relationships, moral obligations, and individual growth. It's about managing the silent struggles and the visible impacts, the subtle tensions and the pronounced conflicts, the unspoken understandings and the spoken disagreements. It's about finding the equilibrium between the financial shadows of the past and the illuminating lessons of the present, all while maintaining the harmony within familial bonds and ensuring the continuity of individual and collective journeys towards financial prudence and stability.

In these silent battles and visible strains, the learning curve has been steep, marked by moments of reflection, realizations, and re-alignments. The threads of financial prudence woven by my grandmother have been the guiding lights, helping navigate through the tempests of financial uncertainties and the landscapes of familial obligations. It's a continual process, a journey marked by the footprints of resilience, adaptation, and growth, with the echoes of the past shaping the symphonies of the present and the future.

Navigating through the tumultuous terrains of financial instability and familial discord has been an expedition steeped in reflection, learning, and growth. The intricate tapestry of my financial journey is woven with threads of contemplation and realization, where the echoes of past indiscretions meet the harmonious tunes of newfound financial wisdom and maturity. Each step in this journey, marked by shadows and light, has been a steppingstone toward financial reconciliation and familial harmony, guiding me through the corridors of self-discovery and transformation.

The silent whispers of financial unrest and familial strains have been constant companions, shaping my perspectives, values, and approaches toward money management and relationships. These whispers have etched profound imprints on my soul, creating a rich canvas of introspections and revelations, painting my journey with hues of resilience, adaptability, and continual growth. It's within these whispers that the essence of my financial metamorphosis and familial bonds have found their true resonance, crafting a harmonious symphony of reflections and evolutions.

The strain of debt on relationships and family dynamics is a complex tapestry, woven with the threads of financial stress, emotional tensions, and moral obligations. It's a journey through the landscapes of familial bonds, financial responsibilities, and personal growth, marked with the footprints of struggles, resilience, and learning. Navigating through this intricate maze requires a balance of understanding, communication, resilience, and, above all, love. It's a dance between the shadows and the light, between the silences and the echoes, between the past and the future, shaping the symphony of our familial bonds and our individual journeys.

Shame, guilt, and secrecy around debt

Debt carries with it a heavy cloak, woven with threads of shame, guilt, and often veiled in layers of secrecy. This burden is not just financial; it deeply infiltrates our psyche, imposing a silent but ever-present whispering shadow, casting doubts, fueling insecurities, and fostering a pervasive sense of isolation. The shame and guilt surrounding debt are colossal, darkening the realms of our existence with a haunting resonance, creating a silent battlefield where the inner turmoil is as real as the numbers accumulating on the ledger.

These silent shadows walk with us, intertwining with our every step, whispering words of self-reproach and remorse, clouding our judgment, distorting our perceptions, and isolating us in a fortress of solitude and secrecy. The sting of guilt permeates our interactions, and the cloak of shame envelops us, creating a labyrinth of silence where the echoes of unspoken words reverberate with the rhythms of concealed pain.

In my journey, the shadow of debt has been a constant companion, whispering tales of guilt, wrapping me in a cloak of shame, and pushing me into the secret corners of financial struggles. Every unpaid bill, every accumulating interest, was a reminder of my financial imprudence, a silent echo of my inability to manage my financial responsibilities adequately. The shame was palpable, a constant weight pressing upon my conscience, reinforcing my feelings of inadequacy and imprudence.

The secrecy around my debt was my shield, my armor against the judging eyes and the pointed fingers. It was my refuge, my silent sanctuary where I could hide my financial flaws, mask my monetary misjudgments, and conceal my fiscal failings. But this sanctuary was also my prison, my solitary confinement where the walls were adorned with the shadows of my financial follies, the air was thick with the whispers of my monetary mistakes, and the silence was broken by the echoes of my fiscal failures.

With every debt I accumulated, I wove a web of secrecy and deception. To friends, I hid the reality of my financial overreaches, painting a picture of comfort even when going over budget. To my parents, I downplayed my earnings, shielding them from the uncomfortable truth that I might be outpacing them financially. My grandmother, who had been my guiding light in understanding finances, received cushioned truths. I minimized the gravity of my debts to her, not wanting to face the disappointment I feared I'd see in her eyes or endure the lectures I knew would follow. Each lie, each omission, carried its weight — a burden of shame, guilt, and deceit. Depending on the audience, my facade shifted, but the internal struggle remained consistent. The weight of the debt and the tangled web of lies it fostered often left me mentally drained, staring at my financial abyss and calculating the future sacrifices it entailed.

The guilt was a relentless companion, walking beside me, reminding me of every financial misstep, whispering words of self-reproach and regret. Every unpaid bill was a sting, every accumulating debt was a slash, cutting through my soul, leaving scars of remorse and regret. The guilt was not just a feeling; it was a living entity, a silent specter haunting my steps, shadowing my existence, and permeating my being.

The interplay of shame, guilt, and secrecy around my debt was a dance of shadows, a silent symphony of concealed pain and unspoken regret. It was a battle, a continuous struggle between the desire for financial redemption and the need for emotional salvation, between the pursuit of fiscal prudence and the quest for psychological peace.

Emerging from the shadows of shame, guilt, and secrecy surrounding debt is not just a financial endeavor; it is an emotional and psychological journey towards self-acceptance, self-forgiveness, and self-liberation. It's about removing the cloak of shame, dispelling the shadows of guilt, and breaking the chains of secrecy. It's about finding the light, the illumination that pierces through the darkness, revealing the path towards financial freedom and emotional liberation.

Breaking the silence surrounding debt is the first step towards shattering the fortress of solitude and secrecy. It's about voicing the unspoken, revealing the concealed, and sharing the isolated. It's about creating a symphony of shared experiences, a harmonious dance of collective struggles, and a united journey towards financial enlightenment and emotional empowerment.

For many, the shadows may still linger, the whispers may still echo, and the fortress may still stand. But the journey towards light has begun, the path towards liberation is being paved, and the symphony of shared experiences is playing its harmonious tunes, resonating with the echoes of shared pains, shared struggles, and shared hopes, all converging into a collective journey towards financial freedom and emotional liberation.

The vicious cycle: Stress leading to more debt

Debt is like quicksand; the more you struggle, the deeper you sink. It entangles individuals in a relentless cycle where stress begets more debt, and more debt fuels further stress. This vicious cycle is not merely a fiscal entrapment; it is a psychological labyrinth, where every turn seems to lead to more despair, every step seems to deepen the financial quagmire, and every effort seems to tighten the fiscal shackles. The stress of existing debts makes individuals more vulnerable, pushing them to make decisions out of desperation and fear, perpetuating a relentless loop of financial despair.

This relentless cycle is perpetuated by a combination of financial constraints, psychological distress, and a lack of financial literacy. The stress induced by existing debts clouds judgment and impairs decision-making abilities, making individuals susceptible to further financial missteps. It is a convoluted web, where the strands of fiscal despair intertwine with the threads of psychological turmoil, creating a tapestry of entangled emotions and intertwined financial struggles.

Breaking free from the cycle of debt and stress has been a challenging journey for many, myself included. The weight of existing debts clouded my judgment, shackling my thoughts with the chains of financial despair. Every decision, every step seemed to be shadowed by the looming specter of financial instability, whispering words of fear and uncertainty, casting doubts, and deepening my sense of fiscal entrapment.

The strain of financial struggles led to a constant state of anxiety and worry, which paradoxically drove me to accrue more debt. The idea of acquiring immediate relief, be it through retail therapy or other means, seemed like an oasis in my financial desert. However, the immediate relief was fleeting, a mirage that vanished, leaving me deeper in the sands of financial despair. The stress emanating from the looming debts perpetuated a state of constant worry and fear, narrowing my vision, impairing my judgment, and deepening my fiscal quagmire.

Each moment of stress and financial strain created a yearning for a reprieve, and, ironically, that reprieve often came in the form of spending beyond my means. Lengthy stretches of disciplined financial restraint, devoid of any personal indulgence, would culminate in moments of weakness. I'd give in, longing for a taste of fun or entertainment. This "live for the moment" mindset, although providing a brief escape from the monotonous grind and looming debt, ironically only plunged me deeper into financial turmoil. It wasn't just the weight of financial obligations that pushed me to this cycle; external stressors – work tensions, family disputes, or even the vicarious effects of someone else's bad day – often led to impulsive spending. These purchases, aimed at instant gratification and mood elevation, were like quick fixes; they felt good momentarily but only intensified the debt spiral I was caught in.

The perpetual cycle of stress and debt was not merely a series of unfortunate financial decisions; it was a psychological battle, a continuous struggle between my rational mind and my emotional impulses. The rational mind understood the importance of financial prudence, the need to break free from the chains of debt, and the urgency to escape the labyrinth of financial despair. However, the emotional impulses, fueled by the stress of existing debts, sought immediate relief, temporary solace, and fleeting respite.

The effort to break free from the cycle of stress and debt has been a journey of self-discovery, self-reflection, and self-transformation. It has been a path of learning, understanding, and evolving, where every step, every turn has been a lesson, a revelation, and a transformation. The struggle to escape the entangled web of financial despair and psychological turmoil has been a battle, a war between the mind and the heart, the rational and the emotional, the prudent and the impulsive.

Escaping the vicious cycle of stress leading to more debt is a multifaceted endeavor, involving not just financial restructuring and fiscal discipline, but also psychological resilience and emotional intelligence. It requires a holistic approach, integrating financial literacy, emotional awareness, and psychological strength, forging a path towards fiscal freedom and emotional liberation.

It is essential to acknowledge the intertwined nature of financial struggles and psychological distress, to understand the convoluted interplay between fiscal constraints and emotional impulses, and to recognize the entangled web of financial and emotional strands. Only by unraveling the intertwined threads of financial and emotional entanglement can one truly escape the vicious cycle of stress leading to more debt.

To genuinely break free from the relentless loop, one must cultivate financial literacy, foster emotional resilience, and develop psychological strength. It is a journey of learning and unlearning, of building and rebuilding, and of transforming and evolving. It is about finding the light amidst the shadows, discovering the path amidst the labyrinth, and forging the way amidst the quicksand.

The journey out of the vicious cycle of stress leading to more debt is a journey of hope, resilience, and transformation. It is a beacon of light in the darkness of financial despair, a beacon of hope in the turmoil of psychological distress, and a beacon of transformation in the labyrinth of emotional turmoil. It is a path towards financial freedom, emotional liberation, and psychological empowerment, leading to a future of fiscal stability, emotional balance, and psychological strength.

Mental health implications: depression, anxiety, and even suicidal thoughts

The silent war that rages within the minds of those engulfed by debt is a battle marked not by outward scars, but by the internal wounds of depression, anxiety, and, at times, thoughts so dark they whisper of ending it all. Debt, a relentless foe, infiltrates the sanctity of the mind, eroding peace and seeding turmoil, sowing the shadows of despair and watering the roots of mental anguish. It is not merely a matter of numbers and balances, but a profound, encompassing distress that impacts every facet of life, every moment of existence, and every fiber of one's being.

The mental health implications of debt are severe, resonating through the caverns of the mind with echoes of shame, guilt, and inadequacy. The psychological burden doesn't merely whisper; it shouts, it screams, it reverberates, adding layers of emotional pain to the tangible financial strain. Depression and anxiety become constant companions to those wading through the murky waters of financial instability, tightening their grip with each passing day, deepening the shadows and heightening the silence that accompanies such unseen struggles.

The descent into the caverns of depression and anxiety, facilitated by the chains of overwhelming debt, is a path I've traversed, with each step weighed down by the heaviness of financial despair. The shadows cast by mounting obligations whispered narratives of failure and inadequacy, while the unrelenting grip of anxiety turned every thought into a battlefield, every moment into a skirmish, every breath into a struggle.

The anxiety manifested not merely as a whispering worry but as a relentless roar, a constant companion whispering tales of impending doom, accentuating every heartbeat with the rhythm of financial despair. The chains of debt became the chains of my existence, shackling my thoughts, imprisoning my mind, and ensnaring my soul in a dance with darkness, a waltz with worry, a symphony of silence.

And within this symphony, the thoughts turned darker, the shadows grew deeper, the silence became louder. The whispers of ending the pain, of silencing the roar, of escaping the chains grew in intensity, becoming a chorus of darkness within the symphony of my existence. It was a battle within, a silent war with unseen wounds, a struggle with unvoiced pain.

It was within this labyrinth of mental anguish that the realization dawned; the realization that breaking the chains of debt required not just fiscal prudence but mental resilience, not just financial discipline but psychological strength. The journey towards financial freedom became a journey towards mental liberation, the path to fiscal stability became the path to psychological peace, the battle with financial despair became the battle with mental shadows.

To break free from the clutches of debt-induced mental health challenges, acknowledging the depth and intensity of the emotional and psychological strife is paramount. It is about embracing vulnerability, seeking support, fostering resilience, and cultivating a mindset of hope and healing. The shadows may be deep, the silence may be loud, but the light of resilience, the melody of hope, can pierce through the darkness, can break through the silence.

Unveiling the unseen battle, breaking the silence of the unvoiced pain, and illuminating the shadows of the unrelenting struggle is the key to untangling the intertwined threads of financial and mental despair. It is a journey of illumination, a journey of voice, a journey of hope. It is about redefining the narratives, rewriting the symphony, reshaping the dance.

In conclusion, the unseen battle with debt's mental health implications is a profound struggle, marked by internal wounds and unvoiced pain. It is a journey through shadows and silence, through depression and anxiety, through unseen wounds and unrelenting struggles. However, it is also a journey of hope and healing, of resilience and renewal, of light and liberation. It is about emerging from the shadows, breaking the silence, and finding the light within, the voice within, the hope within.

THE PHYSCIAL MANIFESTATIONS OF DEBT-STRESS

Stress-related illnesses: heart disease, diabetes, etc.s of Debt and its Evolution

The perilous journey through the quagmire of debt is fraught with more than just financial ramifications; it ventures into the realms of physical health, beckoning many stress-induced ailments. The persistent anxiety associated with mounting debt can catalyze a spectrum of health conditions, transmuting psychological distress into tangible physiological afflictions. It is critical to fathom the intertwining strands of financial stress and its palpable impact on the body, to comprehend the multifarious ways in which our physical well-being is contingent upon our fiscal stability.

A plethora of studies corroborate the profound connection between chronic stress and numerous health conditions, illustrating how the labyrinth of financial strain can entrap one's physiological equilibrium. Chronic stress, especially emanating from enduring financial instability, disrupts the body's homeostasis, unbalancing the intricate symphony of biological processes and propelling the emergence of diverse health maladies.

The human body is endowed with an intricate stress response system, primarily orchestrated by hormones like cortisol and adrenaline. This system is meticulously designed to respond to immediate threats, engendering the well-known fight-or-flight response. However, when this response is perpetually activated by persistent financial stress, it initiates a cascade of detrimental effects, ushering in a state of chronic stress. The relentless secretion of stress hormones results in a sustained state of heightened alertness and physiological arousal, inflicting wear and tear on multiple bodily systems.

Chronic financial stress prolongs the activation of the fight-or-flight response, subjecting the body to continuous exposure to stress hormones. This unabated stress hampers the body's recuperative capabilities, inducing health issues and exacerbating pre-existing conditions, elucidating the insidious nature of financial stress on the human body.

The toll of financial stress is more than just psychological; it manifests tangibly in my physical health. With each bout of stress, my muscles tighten, sleep becomes elusive, and my concentration dwindles. The persistent aches in my upper back and neck, coupled with diminished energy, become pronounced reminders of my internal struggles. This physical degradation often leads me towards unhealthy eating habits, gravitating towards fatty, comfort foods. Consequently, the fusion of mental and physical strain not only saps my motivation but leaves me vulnerable. My body, weakened by the cumulative impact of stress, becomes a ready host for illnesses. When sickness takes hold, it is debilitating. Bedridden with fever, chills, and an overwhelming lethargy, even the smallest tasks seem Herculean. And as the days pass, the mounting backlog of work and missed commitments add yet another layer of stress, creating a daunting cycle that often feels insurmountable.

Chronic stress is a clandestine architect of cardiovascular ailments, stealthily crafting the foundations for heart diseases, hypertension, and elevated cholesterol levels. The persistent anxiety associated with financial instability is a potent catalyst for cardiovascular issues, elevating the risk factors associated with heart conditions. The enduring release of stress hormones, coupled with the inflammation and endothelial dysfunction it induces, are pivotal in the development of atherosclerosis and subsequent heart diseases.

Numerous studies depict a stark correlation between financial stress and an augmented risk of heart conditions. The intertwining strands of economic pressure and heart health are undeniable, underscoring the urgency to mitigate financial stress as a conduit to safeguard cardiovascular well-being.

The body's metabolic machinery is particularly susceptible to the insidious impacts of chronic stress. Persistent financial strain can alter metabolic processes, paving the way for metabolic syndrome, diabetes, and obesity. The stress-induced alterations in metabolic functions can prompt the body to store more fat, particularly in the abdominal region, elevating the risk of developing metabolic disorders.

Moreover, the lifestyle choices concomitant with financial stress accentuate the risk of metabolic conditions. The propensity to indulge in unhealthy dietary habits, coupled with a sedentary lifestyle due to stress, act as accelerants in the progression of metabolic diseases. The relentless cycle of financial stress and unhealthy lifestyle choices perpetuates the risk of developing diabetes and other metabolic disorders, spotlighting the critical interplay between financial well-being and metabolic health.

Chronic financial stress casts its shadow on the gastrointestinal system as well, spurring the onset of conditions like irritable bowel syndrome (IBS), gastritis, and gastroesophageal reflux disease (GERD). The enduring stress elicits alterations in gastrointestinal motility, secretion, and permeability, culminating in diverse gastrointestinal ailments. The stress-induced perturbations in gut microbiota further amplify the risk of gastrointestinal disorders.

The intricate nexus between stress and gastrointestinal health necessitates a holistic approach, assimilating stress management as an integral component in the treatment and prevention of gastrointestinal conditions. The recognition and mitigation of financial stress are indispensable in circumventing the deleterious impacts on gastrointestinal health.

The persistent onslaught of financial stress compromises the body's immune defenses, rendering it more susceptible to infections and protracting the healing process. Chronic stress suppresses the immune response by modulating the release of immune cells and inflammatory cytokines, hampering the body's ability to ward off infections.

Financial stress-induced immune suppression delineates the propensity to succumb to infections and illnesses with increased frequency and severity. The imperatives of maintaining financial equanimity become ever so glaring in light of the impact of fiscal stress on the immune system, underscoring the essence of financial wellness in bolstering immune resilience.

The intersectionality of mental and physical health is a realm of profound implications, delineating the interconnectedness and mutual influence of psychological and physiological well-being. Mental health conditions, intensified by chronic financial stress, can manifest in physical symptoms and contribute to the development of various illnesses. The multifaceted interplay between mental health and physical health is manifested through diverse pathways, including hormonal imbalances, inflammatory responses, and behavioral patterns.

Understanding the symbiotic relationship between mental and physical health in the context of financial stress is pivotal in orchestrating holistic interventions. Addressing the psychological dimensions of financial stress is integral in mitigating its repercussions on physical health, fostering a harmonious balance between mental and physiological well-being.

The sanctity of sleep is incessantly besieged by the relentless tides of financial stress, inducing disorders like insomnia. Sleep, a cornerstone of physical health, is critically modulated by stress levels, and disturbances in sleep patterns can precipitate various health conditions. The circadian disruption and decreased sleep quality induced by financial stress are formidable risk factors for diverse health issues, including cardiovascular diseases, metabolic disorders, and cognitive impairments.

The paramount importance of safeguarding sleep quality amidst financial turmoil is underscored by the myriad of health repercussions associated with sleep disturbances. The pursuit of financial stability is concomitant with the imperative to maintain optimal sleep patterns, fostering physical well-being and cognitive function.

The vortex of financial stress propels individuals towards unhealthy lifestyle choices and maladaptive coping mechanisms, such as excessive alcohol consumption, smoking, and poor diet. These deleterious lifestyle choices accentuate the risk of developing various health conditions, adding another layer to the multidimensional impact of financial stress on physical health. The unhealthy coping strategies not only magnify the physical health risks but also entrench individuals deeper into the quagmire of financial instability.

The pivotal role of lifestyle choices in the context of financial stress accentuates the necessity of cultivating healthy coping mechanisms and lifestyle habits. The cultivation of resilience, healthy lifestyle habits, and adaptive coping strategies is integral in mitigating the physical health impacts of financial stress and fostering overall well-being.

Mitigating the physical repercussions of financial stress necessitates a multipronged approach, incorporating lifestyle modifications, stress management interventions, and financial literacy. Fostering financial well-being is integral in alleviating the physical manifestations of financial stress, underscoring the essence of financial education and management in promoting overall health.

Holistic interventions, incorporating both mental and physical health dimensions, are crucial in navigating the multifaceted impacts of financial stress. The exploration and integration of stress-reduction techniques, healthy lifestyle choices, and financial management strategies are pivotal in orchestrating a harmonious balance between financial stability and physical well-being.

The intricate tapestry of financial stress weaves through the realms of physical health, etching its imprints on the physiological symphony of the human body. The myriad of health conditions emerging from the shadows of financial instability illustrates the profound interconnection between fiscal and physiological well-being. The myriad of physical manifestations of debt stress, ranging from cardiovascular ailments to immune suppression, underscores the urgent imperatives of addressing financial stress as a public health concern.

The journey through the labyrinth of financial stress and its physical manifestations necessitates a holistic compass, integrating mental health, physical health, and financial well-being. The strategies for mitigation and prevention of the physical impacts of financial stress delineate the path towards a harmonious confluence of financial stability and holistic well-being, fostering a future where the shadows of financial instability no longer veil the sanctity of human health.

This exploration of the physical manifestations of debt-stress illuminates the multifarious dimensions of the human experience amidst financial turbulence, providing a beacon of understanding and awareness in the intricate interplay between financial stress and physical health.

Poor health habits exacerbated by financial strain

The relentless grasp of financial strain subtly coerced my life into a cascade of detrimental health habits and neglected well-being. Each morning was a symphony of exhaustion, an encounter with the day that, regardless of the slumber's length, was marred with fatigue. At 6:30, the alarm's call was the herald of another journey through hours of weariness, draped in an overarching lack of energy and vitality.

The choices I made in terms of sustenance were reflective of the fiscal constraints shadowing my days. The illusion of affordability in fast, processed foods became my refuge, a seemingly necessary compromise within the looming realm of financial instability. These daily compromises were the invisible chains binding my well-being, leading to a countenance marked by acne and a vitality constantly on the wane, rendering the reflection in the mirror a painful reminder of a life consumed by financial turmoil.

Every meal became a voyage through the terrains of compromised nutrition, a stroll amidst the aisles of unhealthy temptations. The elusive energy seemed a fleeting companion in this journey, leaving in its wake a soul embattled with fatigue and a body echoing the strains of unwholesome living. The mirror reflected not just my external appearance but served as a silent echo of internal neglect, a manifestation of the intertwined realms of financial instability and compromised health.

Amid the weight of financial burdens and tumultuous emotions, there was another, more visible weight I began to bear: my physical weight. Back in my youth, blessed with a rapid metabolism and a penchant for spicy foods, maintaining a svelte figure had been almost effortless. But by the fall of 2022, the mirror no longer reflected that young, energetic version of myself. One particular photograph from a music festival with my fiancée made the change strikingly evident – fuller cheeks, a protruding belly, and a shirt that clung tighter than ever before. Weighing 175 pounds, the BMI scale might have deemed me 'in the clear', yet I couldn't shake off the feeling of that impending "dad bod". It wasn't just about aesthetics – I felt the physical drag: a beer too many made my steps heavy, stairs became challenges, and my energy flagged.

However, in the lead-up to our engagement, I resolved to reclaim my health. Embracing regular workouts and a revamped diet, I battled both the physical inertia and the mental lows from resisting unhealthy food temptations. Admittedly, the financial strain sometimes tempted me to splurge on a lavish, unhealthy meal, seeking comfort amidst the financial chaos. But by January 2023, consistency in healthy eating became my creed. Years of financial missteps had translated into years of neglecting my health: opting for convenience over nourishment, lethargy over activity, and digital screens over active pursuits. Today, armed with newfound financial knowledge and a commitment to my well-being, I'm not just on a path to fiscal recovery, but physical rejuvenation. The vitality I feel now fuels not only my body but my determination to tackle debts head-on.

For me, dental visits felt less like a regular health check and more like an economic tug-of-war. I'd think, "Do I want to part with even a penny when I'm already in this financial quagmire?" Thus, dental check-ups turned into rare occurrences, spanning years of oversight. In reality, this evasion to save money became a costly oversight. My negligence came to a head when a neglected tooth wreaked havoc, culminating in intense pain. With insurance covering only a fraction of the procedure, I found myself paying $3,000 out-of-pocket. Yet, the fiscal nightmare didn't end there. Two years later, I was blindsided by a collections agency calling about an outstanding $2,000 – a result of the dentist's administrative oversight with insurance details. My attempt to avoid short-term expenses due to existing debt led to long-term, exacerbated financial strains.

Dental hygiene, a seemingly mundane but crucial aspect of health, became a silent casualty in my relentless battle with financial constraints. The lack of budget allocation for this vital aspect of well-being became the precursor to a painful and costly confrontation with dental issues. The discomfort, initially dismissed, morphed into a painful reminder of neglected health, necessitating an unforeseen and unbudgeted dental intervention that amounted to over $3,000 for an implant.

The ordeal of addressing a dead tooth and its subsequent financial impact was a relentless echo of the ever-present financial strain, unraveling in monthly payments that seemed to perpetually extend the shadows of fiscal instability in my life. This encounter was not just a painful experience but also a glaring reminder of the integral connection between financial stability and holistic well-being.

The journey through this phase was more than just a personal struggle; it was a reflection of the pervasive influence of financial instability on our lives and choices. My experiences were but echoes of the untold stories of countless others, navigating the turbulent waters of financial strain and its subsequent impact on well-being. The compromised nutrition, the neglected dental health, and the overarching weariness were silent testimonies to the unseen and often unspoken repercussions of living in the shadows of financial uncertainty.

The intertwined strands of financial instability and poor health habits are a silent narrative, painting our lives with the hues of neglected well-being and unheeded health. This relentless cycle is a poignant reminder of the multifaceted impact of financial strain on our choices, our habits, and our overall sense of well-being. The echoes of unwholesome choices and the silent tales of neglected health whisper the untold narratives of life under the silent siege of financial instability.

This intricate tapestry of experiences serves as a reflection on the relationship between financial well-being and overall health. It is a journey through the shadows of neglected health, a silent testimony to the untold stories of struggle and compromise that unfold in the realm of financial strain. The echoes of this journey reverberate in the myriad tales of compromised well-being and unheeded wake-up calls, whispering the silent stories of life amidst the turbulent waters of financial uncertainty.

The relationship between debt and substance abuse

The intricate relationship between debt and substance abuse is a profound and complex one, weaving a tapestry of physical and psychological strains that many grapple with. Substantive research and anecdotal evidence both point towards a tangible connection between financial distress and an increased susceptibility to substance abuse. It's a dance of despair where one fuels the other in a perpetual and destructive cycle.

Debt, inherently a source of unrelenting stress and anxiety, creates an environment fertile for escapism, and unfortunately, this escapism is often found in the form of substance abuse. This dynamic arises from the human tendency to seek relief from relentless mental distress, leading to reliance on substances as a means to temporarily numb the pain and escape the omnipresent weight of financial burden. In the vortex of this escapism, the immediate relief shadows the long-term consequences, creating a deceptive sanctuary in the storm of financial woes.

Personally, I often ponder how different my life might have been without the vivid memories of my father's smoking habit and the devastating stroke it led to. Those experiences ingrained in me an aversion to cigarettes and the detrimental effects they carry. The pungent smoke, difficult to inhale and escape from, has always been a source of discomfort. I recall instances in the car, gasping for fresh air or opening a window whenever my father lit up. These memories persist. Even today, I find myself distancing from smokers on the streets, either pausing to let the air clear or hastening my steps to steer clear of the smoke. My upbringing, coupled with my father's health struggles, instilled in me not just an aversion to smoking but a broader perspective on substance abuse. While my way of coping with financial stress leaned towards buying with debt, I recognize that some spiral down the path of substance abuse, a perilous avenue that I fortunately bypassed due to my formative experiences.

When individuals find themselves entrenched in debt, the constant worry and the feeling of helplessness can drive them towards substances as a means of coping. The use of alcohol, drugs, or other substances can, momentarily, provide a refuge from the reality of mounting bills, looming deadlines, and the ever-present shadow of insolvency. It's a precarious balance, a momentary respite that engenders a myriad of long-term implications, exacerbating the very circumstances it seeks to alleviate.

Substance abuse, in turn, contributes to the deterioration of one's financial situation. The costs associated with purchasing substances, coupled with the potential loss of employment due to impaired performance or attendance issues, can magnify the financial strain. This escalating cycle of substance abuse and debt can erode one's physical and mental well-being, rendering them vulnerable to a spectrum of health issues and psychosocial impairments.

Moreover, the interaction between debt and substance abuse extends its tendrils into familial and social relationships, straining bonds and isolating individuals. The secrecy, guilt, and shame enveloping substance abuse and financial distress form a cocoon of isolation, pushing away loved ones and support networks, and deepening the spiral of despair and dependency.

Addressing this multifaceted relationship necessitates a holistic approach, focusing on both financial and mental well-being. Intervention strategies need to encompass financial counseling, mental health support, and substance abuse treatment, aiming to dismantle the vicious cycle and restore equilibrium in the lives of those entangled in this intricate dance of despair.

The interplay between debt and substance abuse is a profound manifestation of the human struggle with distress and escape. It's a silent epidemic, speaking volumes in the echoes of its aftermath, whispering tales of struggle, escape, and the enduring hope for respite and recovery. It underlines the imperativeness of awareness, holistic intervention, and sustained support to untangle the intricate webs of debt and dependency, paving the path towards healing and reconciliation.

Debt's role in career choices and work stress

Navigating through the labyrinth of debt is not merely a financial journey; it has profound implications on career choices and induces significant work stress. When entangled in the strings of debt, one often finds themselves standing at the crossroads, facing the daunting choice between passion and necessity. It is the silent orchestrator behind the scenes, compelling individuals to prioritize financial stability over the pursuit of their true calling, creating an atmosphere saturated with stress, regret, and unfulfillment.

I launched myself into the professional stratosphere as an accounting assistant, where the rhythm of my days was composed of numbers and financial nuances, earning a steady 46K annually. For 6-7 long months, my reality was cloaked in routine, every day mirroring the mundane tasks of the last, the monotony punctuated only by the fleeting specters of growth, which seemed distant and elusive. The sameness of my days started weaving threads of discontent, the thirst for evolution and growth becoming a persistent companion in my thoughts.

It was during this professional quandary that destiny intervened, reshaping my journey unexpectedly. A coworker, who soon morphed into a cherished friend, encountered a misfortune, tearing his ACL. This twist of fate led me to inherit his responsibilities.

Recognizing the opportunity, I willingly took on the extra work, often staying late to ensure tasks were completed and projects remained on track. My dedication and effort did not go unnoticed. As I seamlessly transitioned into the realm of a Project Engineer for the Electrical Contractor I worked at, the management recognized my potential and extended an invitation to join the Projects Management Team. It was not just a switch in roles but a leap toward financial elevation, with my annual income experiencing a significant surge to 100K over the ensuing five years.

Simultaneously, my creative passions were finding their voice on a platform that was burgeoning as a digital sensation—TikTok. What commenced as a mere dalliance with content creation, focusing predominantly on video game themes, evolved into a successful venture. My digital expressions found resonance and camaraderie among a diverse audience, my follower count swelling to an impressive 60K, with my content receiving over 5 million likes.

The success and fulfillment derived from my creative exploits on TikTok became the beacon of my aspirational journey, whispering to my heart the possibility of aligning my professional path with my true passion. The realms of social media beckoned me, promising landscapes where my heart could dance in unison with my aspirations. However, the practical world painted a different reality.

I found myself navigating through exhilarating life chapters; amidst my professional journey and digital exploits, the strings of my heart intertwined with those of another, leading to a beautiful tapestry of engagement. The announcement of lifelong companionship with my fiancé heralded not just the celebration of love but also signified a geographical transition—we decided to anchor our lives in LA, the land that resonated as home for my fiancé's family. The horizon of LA painted a canvas of new beginnings, familial bonds, and the hope of a harmonious marital odyssey.

The prospect of relocation nudged me to delve into the job market anew, igniting the dormant aspirations of aligning my professional path with my blossoming passion in marketing and social media. The city of angels seemed to whisper promises of synchronicity between my heart's song and my life's work. However, the echoes of reality resonated differently. Even with promising interviews and opportunities in the realm of social media, the figures on the offer letters seemed to dance in a distant melody—salaries, which on paper were encapsulated within the 65K margin, seemed to reflect not the harmonious tunes of passion fulfilled but rather the stern echoes of practicality and responsibility. The numbers, the opportunities, they all seemed to be enmeshed in a dance, one that was far removed from the shadows of the debt accumulated during my days enveloped in a 100K salary.

The voices of unmet financial commitments and obligations reverberated louder than the alluring whispers of passion, painting my canvas with hues of compromises and unfulfilled desires. Thus, the shadows of debt continued to etch their silent stories on the chapters of my life, leading me back to the territories marked by professional skills and familiarity. It was here, amidst the silent echoes of unexplored possibilities, that I embraced a new role in an electrical manufacturing company, seeking solace and pragmatism in a 105K salary.

This intertwining dance between the unrelenting whispers of debt and the fiery essence of unfulfilled desires continues to craft the symphony of my journey, leaving in its wake reflections of sacrifices and the unquenched thirst of untraveled realms. However, the whispered promises collided with the reality of a potential substantial reduction in financial stability. The looming shadows of debt became the unseen barrier, the silent voice of restraint whispering words of caution, overshadowing my flames of passion. The choice became a reflection of the relentless dichotomy between passion and obligation, a tangible representation of the unseen battles fought in the realms of professional decisions.

In the intricate tapestry of my professional journey, each thread represents a silent echo of compromised dreams and untapped potentials, each weave a testament to the relentless dance between financial stability and unbridled passion. The labyrinth of debt and its shadows shape the corridors of professional existences, leaving imprints of sacrifices, of untraveled paths.

Debt, in its silent omnipresence, becomes the unseen sculptor of professional landscapes, molding paths, shaping destinies, and directing courses. The essence of the journey is in the silent wars waged in the shadows of compromises and sacrifices. The symphony of unfulfilled aspirations resonates, underscoring the profound implications of the unseen partner of financial obligations.

I continue to reflect upon the intertwining relationship between debt and career choices, acknowledging the pervasive echoes of unfulfilled dreams and untraveled paths. The eternal dance between ambition and reality goes on, with the hues of dreams, sacrifices, and the ever-looming shadows of financial obligations shaping my journey. They leave behind the echoes of unexplored terrains and untapped potentials in the silent embrace of debt. It is crucial to understand the depth of this intricate relationship between debt and career choices, as it highlights a pervasive dilemma, silently shaping destinies. The shadows of debt linger, whispering tales of compromise and unfulfilled aspirations, emphasizing the need for financial consciousness and the pursuit of a balanced existence. The dance between passion and obligation continues, painting the canvas of professional journeys with the vibrant colors of dreams, realities, and the ever-present silhouette of debt.

The impact on overall life satisfaction and happiness

Life, with its diverse array of colors and shades, often seeks its essence in the pursuit of happiness and satisfaction, elements seemingly abstract but vital to the human spirit. The journey through life's landscapes is significantly influenced by the equilibrium of our emotional and mental states, often reflecting the interplay between our internal world and the external circumstances enveloping it. Amidst the ebb and flow of financial circumstances, I've ardently strived to carve out a life of satisfaction and happiness, both in times of financial strain and moments of relief. The allure of instant gratifications from debt provided ephemeral joys, a transient euphoria that would later be shrouded by waves of anxiety. My personal narrative has consistently been a rollercoaster, with highs of achievement and lows dictated by monetary woes. Too often, I've let financial hurdles define my mood, my satisfaction, and my perception of self-worth. While debt momentarily flattered my desires, it inevitably demanded its due, tainting my moments of happiness with looming reminders of obligations. While the essence of my being resonates with an intrinsic positivity, echoing the tunes of optimism and hope, the chains of debt intermittently cast shadows on the canvases of my contentment.

The labyrinth of debt, with its intricate patterns of stress and worry, inevitably brings forth moments where the brightness of optimism dims, causing the vibrations of happiness to wane. The oscillations between the realms of financial burdens and the pursuit of contentment create a dance, one where the steps are often misaligned, leading to a syncopation of the soul's melodies. For every step forward in the dance of life, the shadows of debt, like an unseen partner, pull me a step back, influencing the rhythm of my overall life satisfaction.

The journey through the realms of professional exploration and transitions illustrated the silent impact of debt on my aspirations and choices. The joy derived from creative expressions and digital adventures, where content creation became the brush painting my world with vibrant hues, often found its colors muted by the limitations imposed by financial obligations. The pursuit of passion, a path seemingly aligned with the harmonious tunes of my being, found itself enveloped in the echoes of practicality, steering my steps towards the terrains marked by familiar skills and stable income.

The silent dance between my inherent positive outlook and the persistent shadows of debt narrates a story of resilience and struggle. The moments of joy derived from personal milestones, such as the engagement with my fiancé and the anticipation of building a life together in the city of angels, are intertwined with the subtle strains emanating from financial constraints. The melodies of love and togetherness are often accompanied by the silent notes of compromises and unfulfilled desires, creating a symphony reflecting the complexities of life satisfaction.

In the dance of life, the steps of positivity and optimism are crucial in navigating through the intricate patterns of challenges and uncertainties. While the shadows of debt cast their transient imprints on my journey, the essence of my being continues to resonate with the tunes of hope and resilience. The pursuit of happiness, a journey marked by the interplay between internal resilience and external circumstances, is a continuous exploration, one where the echoes of debt form the silent background music influencing the dance's rhythm.

Ultimately, life satisfaction isn't just shaped by external pressures but also by our inner strength and optimism. My journey, swayed by the balance of debt and happiness, remains a testament to resilience. Each step I take is a brushstroke, painting my life with optimism and contentment.

THE SOCIETAL VIEW OF DEBT

Taboos and stigmas associated with indebtedness

Across diverse cultures, especially those placing a significant emphasis on individualism and self-reliance, indebtedness is frequently seen as a sign of irresponsibility, moral inadequacy, and failure. In such societies, the weight of debt carries with it not just financial ramifications but also social and emotional repercussions. Individuals find themselves entangled not just in financial obligations but also in a web of shame, isolation, and judgment. The silence surrounding discussions on debt perpetuates these stigmas, making it a challenging cycle to break and an even more challenging topic to navigate openly.

Personally, my silence about my own debts was rooted in this very stigma. Acknowledging them felt like admitting that I was not well-versed in money management and personal finance. When debt was ever discussed among peers or family, it wasn't with accurate figures or candid acknowledgment but with vague descriptors like "it's high" or "I've got some." This secretive language reinforced the notion that debt was something to be hidden, further strengthening the chains of shame.

Within the spectrum of societal interactions, debt often becomes a silent player, manipulating relationships and self-perceptions, distorting them through the lens of external and internal judgments. The very presence of debt can render an individual susceptible to societal ridicule, as many view indebtedness as a direct consequence of imprudent financial decisions, lack of self-control, and moral shortcomings. It's often perceived as a manifestation of personal inadequacy, indicative of a flawed character unable to navigate the currents of financial responsibility.

The stigmas and taboos woven around debt are embodied in everyday interactions and discussions. Hushed whispers accompany the mention of bankruptcy, and a subtle air of superiority colors interactions with those who openly speak about their financial struggles. These stigmas manifest in tangible feelings of shame, guilt, and embarrassment, leading individuals to cloak their financial difficulties in secrecy, avoiding discussions about their monetary challenges even with close family and friends. The consequence is an ongoing cycle of isolation, where the lack of open dialogue exacerbates feelings of alienation and helplessness.

In a society deeply entrenched in consumerist values, the paradox between the normalization of debt and the accompanying stigmas becomes glaringly apparent. On one hand, accumulating debt is almost seen as a rite of passage, an inevitable accompaniment to modern living, with credit cards and loans being peddled at every corner. On the other hand, the struggle to repay these debts remains shrouded in silence, creating an environment ripe for judgment and misconception.

Many cultural narratives depict debt as the result of reckless spending and frivolous desires, ignoring the complex and often unavoidable circumstances leading to indebtedness. Medical emergencies, sudden loss of employment, student loans—these are just a few of the unavoidable realities pushing individuals into the vortex of debt. The prevailing societal narrative, however, focuses on self-inflicted financial wounds, overshadowing the instances where debt was the last resort, not a thoughtless choice.

The reluctance to speak openly about debt and its impacts accentuates the taboos surrounding it. The societal pressure to portray a façade of financial stability and success leads to a collective denial of the struggles intertwined with indebtedness. It creates a dichotomy between the perceived self and the actual self, where individuals, in an attempt to conform to societal expectations, mask their financial struggles, perpetuating the cycle of silence and shame.

The media and popular culture, too, play pivotal roles in perpetuating stigmas surrounding debt. The portrayals of indebted individuals often oscillate between the extremes of reckless spendthrifts and pitiable victims, rarely delving into the complexities of financial struggles. The absence of nuanced representation reinforces stereotypes, solidifying the prevailing notions of irresponsibility and inadequacy associated with debt.

Moreover, the educational systems, by largely neglecting financial literacy, inadvertently contribute to the taboos surrounding debt. The lack of comprehensive education on managing finances, understanding debts, and navigating the intricacies of financial decisions leaves individuals ill-equipped to handle their finances, making them more vulnerable to falling into the debt trap.

Over time, I came to realize a deeply rooted misconception that permeated my understanding of debt: the idea that merely paying the minimum balance was sufficient. This belief paints a false picture, suggesting that one can indulge in purchases well beyond their means and still be financially stable. Even when aware of the compounding effects of interest, many individuals, myself included, might shrug it off, often resorting to minimum payments. Though I was well-informed about the pitfalls of sticking solely to the minimum payments and the merits of paying off most or all of the balance every statement cycle, there were moments where I succumbed to this mindset. In instances where multiple lines of credit beckoned, I'd often focus on clearing one debt entirely, relegating others to the bare minimum payment just to avert additional charges.

In delving into the intricate patterns of societal taboos and stigmas surrounding debt, it's crucial to remember that these constructs often reflect generalized and stereotypical viewpoints rather than the complex reality of indebtedness. The judgments and misconceptions about those in debt often overshadow the numerous circumstances, unanticipated hardships, and systemic issues leading individuals into financial turmoil. Breaking the silence around debt and fostering a more empathetic and nuanced conversation is essential in demystifying the societal shadows cloaking debt. It is a step towards alleviating the shame associated with it, thus empowering individuals to seek guidance, share their experiences, and collectively work towards financial well-being and understanding.

The dialogue surrounding debt is often ensnared in a web of judgments and misconceptions. Society frequently paints a picture of those in debt with a broad brush, insinuating mismanagement, lack of foresight, or even reckless spending habits, while neglecting the plethora of reasons that people might find themselves in such a predicament. From the sudden loss of employment, medical emergencies, to the simple desire of obtaining an education, the paths to indebtedness are manifold and nuanced. These generalized misconceptions create an environment where moral and character assessments are, albeit inaccurately, intertwined with one's financial stability, perpetuating an undue stigma that shadows debt.

Debt, initially presenting itself as a mere tool for credit building, gradually morphed into an insidious presence in my life, subtly escalating from a manageable burden to a looming threat. My early understanding painted debt as a benign entity, a means to pursue higher education and thereby, a successful, stable future. Starting my career with a $46K annual salary, my degree in Finance seemed like a logical path towards ensuring financial stability. However, a mere eight months into my accounting role, the realization dawned that not only was I stuck in a field that barely skimmed the surface of my educational expertise, but I was also trapped in a cycle of continuous debt payment that stripped away any semblance of financial freedom.

Despite the dreariness of my financial outlook, when opportunities to indulge in life's pleasures – from travels, new gadgets, to exploring novelties – arose, they were accompanied by a subtle, yet persistent lifestyle creep. Ironically, debt – the very element that should have restrained my expenditures – falsely empowered them instead, allowing me to indulge in future earnings at the mere cost of present indebtedness. While these endeavors brought joy and experience into my life, they also silently fortified the financial shackles, limiting my choices, freedoms, and indeed, my self-perception.

As I embarked on the journey of companionship, envisioning a future with my fiancé, a stark contrast between our financial states emerged. Here I was, encapsulated in debt, while my partner stood financially stable and secure. Her debt-free status, juxtaposed against my continual financial struggle, augmented my internal turmoil. The question that relentlessly lingered in the back of my mind was: what was I bringing into our future together? The disparity between my ambitions and my financial reality bore heavily upon me, relegating my self-assessment to a mere reflection of my indebtedness. Despite possessing the grit and mental fortitude to persevere, the shadow of debt incessantly lingered, subtly dictating my path and ensuring that, while my ambitions soared, my reality remained tethered to my past financial choices.

The societal lens, through which debt is viewed, often diminishes the reasons and scenarios that lead individuals down this path, submerging them in a sea of judgments and preconceived notions. Dismantling the misjudgments and misconceptions about debt requires a collective effort to embrace empathy, understanding, and a willingness to understand the multitudes of stories and circumstances that have led people into financial instability. Crafting a society that separates a person's worth from their financial standing necessitates a shift in dialogue, policy, and ultimately, in the collective mindset towards debt, guiding us towards a more supportive and equitable framework.

Judgments and misconceptions about those in debt

Judgments and misconceptions about debt create a layered, complex narrative within society. Each individual journey through the path of debt, with its trials and tribulations, unfolds under a broader canopy of societal beliefs, stereotypes, and often unspoken rules about financial management and personal worth. The societal lens through which debt is viewed is, more often than not, frosted with presuppositions and fails to capture the many personal, economic, and situational factors that lead to its accumulation. From the outsider's viewpoint, debt is frequently interpreted as a tangible manifestation of fiscal irresponsibility, frivolity, or lack of foresight. But is it fair? Is it a just synopsis of the lived experiences of countless individuals navigating the turbulent waters of debt management?

Within these assumptions and often harsh judgments, my own story with debt found its genesis and evolution. My initial experiences with debt were, in part, shaped by youthful exuberance and a somewhat naïve understanding of financial intricacies. I recall the time I purchased a motorcycle, opting for a 72-month loan to finance it. My grandmother, wise with years and presumably well-versed in the prudent management of resources, displayed a look of subtle, yet palpable disgust upon learning about the loan. At 22, the dynamics of financial loans, interest, and the prolonged commitment to repayments were concepts I admittedly had not fully grasped.

Although I was confident about managing the repayments, placing more than just the minimum required amount, her judgment lingered, a silent testament to the disconnect that often exists between generational views on financial management and debt. While I believed that by paying more than the monthly payment, I was safeguarding against excessive interest, this perceived cushion inadvertently emboldened me to spend a tad more. The trap lay in believing I had enough for at least the minimum payment, which, over time, incurred more interest than I had anticipated.

Navigating through these financial commitments post-college, I found myself grappling with a plethora of student loans from various providers, each carrying its own unique interest rate. Even my grandmother, with her seasoned understanding of finances, had advised me to consider consolidating my loans. She posited that while it would mean facing a larger principal amount upfront, I could potentially benefit from a reduced interest rate in the long run. This would allow me to streamline my payments and perhaps find some semblance of peace amidst the financial chaos.

However, on top of these student loans, I also had to confront the ubiquitous adversary that is credit card debt. While my student loans hovered comfortably under a 5% interest rate, the towering 19.99% on my credit card stood as a stark contrast. I was meticulous in ensuring it was paid off fully to stave off the paralyzing effects of its high-interest rates.

Interestingly, despite the discussions about consolidation and the pressing advice from my grandmother, youthful indolence, combined with an inherent belief in my individualistic financial strategies, led me to maintain my separate loan accounts. I tended to each in what I believed to be a judicious manner. This approach bore some unexpected fruits when the pandemic hit. The cessation of interest on my federal loans due to Covid allowed me to channel my focus on paying off my private loans. But, there was a flip side to this coin. The hiatus on my federal loan payments, combined with the cessation of interest, resulted in a lack of motivation to continue chipping away at the principal. Rather than taking advantage of this interest-free period, I found myself redirecting the funds that would have gone into debt repayment towards more consumeristic endeavors. So, while my private loans found their closure, my federal loans stagnated, and I found myself ensnared in a fresh web of consumeristic temptations.

My debt journey has been a rather private affair, selectively shared with a few, and strategically veiled from others. As I aged and wisdom gradually began to seep into my financial dealings, I became more forthcoming about my situation with my fiancé, initiating vital dialogues about our fiscal futures.

However, when it came to my family, their insights into my financial landscape were more filtered. My grandmother, whom I held in high regard, only knew select chapters of my debt story. To protect both her sentiments and my own vulnerability, I cushioned the realities of my credit card debt, sidestepping the anticipated disappointment and ire I imagined she would feel. With my parents, I found it easier to speak about my student loans – a form of debt that, while burdensome, carries a societal acceptance, almost seen as a rite of passage for the modern-day graduate.

To further deflect from my actual financial status, I'd often convey the narrative that my finances were primarily occupied with debt repayments. By doing this, I aimed to mask my occasional splurges on gadgets, getaways, and other personal indulgences. By perpetuating the idea that I was continually chipping away at my debt, it gave the illusion of a tighter financial situation, making it less likely for them to suspect or question my more consumeristic expenditures.

Despite having navigated through varied forms of consumer debt, I found empathy to be a scarce commodity within my social and familial circles. More often than not, discussions about debt, particularly those rooted deeply within consumerism, were met with criticism, shaking heads, and a somewhat dismissive "you should have known better" attitude. Although I recklessly rode the waves of consumer debt in my younger years, these reactions failed to comprehend the complexities of my journey, ignoring the systemic and social pressures that often catapult individuals into the abyss of debt.

It's intriguing how personal experiences with debt manage to alter one's perceptions and beliefs about it. My own journey, fraught with its own set of hurdles, nudged me towards a more enlightened and considered approach towards managing finances. Living at home and largely free from substantial financial obligations, my focus shifted towards eradicating my debt, embracing a life that stepped away from relying on 'future money' and instead, placing financial freedom at the forefront of my fiscal strategies. Engaging in this dialogue with myself, setting the ambitious, yet entirely necessary goal to be debt-free before marriage, altered not only my financial behaviors but also fostered personal and professional growth.

I've witnessed disparate generational approaches to debt within my family. My grandmother, who wisely utilized debt as a lever to acquire both residential and commercial properties, showcases a stark contrast to my parents, whose debts were often shackled to consumables and an aspiration to 'keep up with the Joneses'. These dual narratives informed my earlier approaches to debt, oscillating between using borrowed funds for tangible assets and squandering it on transitory items and experiences, attempting to portray an image of affluence and contentment to the external world.

Confronting these views on debt, wrestling with their implications, and ultimately forming my own philosophy towards it has been a nuanced journey. Embracing debt in the future would only be in the context of tangible, appreciating assets, akin to my grandmother's strategy with real estate. Personal items, those depreciating liabilities like cars or the latest technological gadget, would be purchased outright, sans debt, adhering to a learned aversion to unnecessary financial obligations.

Now, when I think of social media, its authenticity is up in the air for me. I often wonder, how many face the same troubles I do with debt while living so lavishly? And on the flip side, how many are genuinely doing financially well? Was I the outlier? The social fabric that weaves through our perceptions and interactions with debt is one that conceals as much as it reveals. Social media, with its curated display of affluence, happiness, and success, rarely unveils the financial realities that lurk behind the images of travel, new cars, and the latest technologies. The individuals portraying these seemingly prosperous lives may well be shackled by debt, a truth seldom shared amidst the polished portrayals of their existence. It raises the question – how many are navigating through similar financial waters, concealing their truths behind a façade of fiscal stability and prosperity?

As I pen down my experiences, reflections, and newfound knowledge in this book, I invite you to ponder upon your own journey, your own perceptions, and perhaps, misconceptions about debt. The narratives we build, both personally and as a collective society, often veer away from reality, casting shadows upon the multifaceted, intricate, and deeply personal stories that weave through each individual's experiences with debt. May we all strive to foster an environment where dialogues about debt are devoid of judgment and replete with understanding, empathy, and a genuine acknowledgment of the myriad paths that lead to its doorstep.

Pop culture and media portrayal of debt

The prevailing narratives of debt in pop culture and media often depict a dichotomy: debt is either glamorized and normalized, often through showcasing lavish lifestyles that are presumably debt-financed, or it is showcased as a perilous situation, typically reserved for cautionary tales. The media's portrayal of debt, particularly in pop culture, undeniably influences societal attitudes toward borrowing, spending, and ultimately, financial management. Television shows, movies, and advertisements often show characters leading opulent lifestyles, with little visible consequence or discussion regarding the financial means through which this lifestyle is achieved. This establishes a subliminal yet pervasive message: the embodiment of a high-end lifestyle, even if debt-financed, is desirable and, perhaps, even expected.

My relationship with debt has been undeniably influenced by social media and its connections to various elements of pop culture, including movies, books, anime, and influencers that revolve around my hobbies, like technology and video games. The endless scrolling brought forth a cascade of items that sparked my interest, and I frequently found myself succumbing to the dopamine hit that came with acquiring the latest, seemingly coolest gadgets or trends presented to me. Several years went by in this manner; my debt accumulating as I consistently gave in to the subtle persuasive power of social media marketing, forever chasing the satisfaction of possessing the latest and greatest.

Interestingly, I noticed a peculiar phenomenon within the realm of social media: a dichotomy of messages, where on one hand there was a glamorization of debt - influencers might leverage 'buy now, pay later' options - and on the other, an influx of ads centered around personal finance, particularly after I delved deeper into that topic. Ads that offered salvation from credit card debt, or suggested debt consolidation, began to emerge, featuring young, relatable individuals, and employing compelling language designed to attract and reassure.

Yet, I found myself somewhat amused by these ads. I had come to realize that escaping the treacherous clutches of debt was no easy journey. It required a degree of resolve, a touch of hard work, and a splash of grit that these ads failed to convey. Their promises were sugar-coated, presenting a somewhat misconstrued perception of the pathway out of debt, which might potentially lead others down a deceptive road where they believe they are alleviating their financial burdens while, in reality, they might be compounding them.

In an era where social media influencers wield considerable impact, wielding their lifestyles as a beacon of aspirational living, the lines between sensible financial management and overindulgence become increasingly blurred. How many times have I seen influencers unbox the latest tech gadgets, wear designer clothing, or travel to exotic locations, only to feel a pang of desire resonating within me? This, in turn, prompted a subtle internal justification that buying those products or emulating that lifestyle, even on credit, was somehow acceptable because it was so commonplace, so glamorized in the digital spaces I inhabited.

The overarching narratives in pop culture, in general, bolster this outlook. Movies and series where characters live in inexplicably luxurious apartments, frequenting high-end restaurants, draped in the latest fashion, all while working seemingly average-paying jobs, breed a subtle yet persistent disconnect between financial reality and the lifestyles we are told we should aspire to lead. This discrepancy generates a climate where living beyond one's means not only becomes normalized but is often actively encouraged, without explicitly doing so.

This leads to crucial reflection: how does one navigate through a society where the limelight is so often cast on the material, the luxurious, and the financially unattainable, without becoming ensnared in the pernicious web of debt and over-consumption? Striking a balance between enjoying the pleasures of contemporary life, whilst maintaining prudent financial health, is no straightforward task, particularly when societal messages are incessantly nudging toward expenditure and financial commitment.

It is imperative to foster a conscious awareness regarding the implicit and explicit messages being conveyed through various media channels. Recognizing that advertisements, influencers, and various pop culture elements are meticulously crafted to entice spending and, at times, indebtedness, is pivotal. Their livelihood often depends on their ability to convince their audience that the products they endorse or the lifestyle they lead is not only desirable but crucial for social acceptance and personal happiness.

Conversely, despite the predominant narratives, a counter-culture exists, albeit less conspicuously. Financial wellness communities, minimalist lifestyles, and advocates for sensible spending are emerging, offering an alternative viewpoint and support in a society so saturated with messages of consumerism. They signify a beacon of resistance against a tide of messages urging us to plunge into financial commitments without thorough consideration of the broader implications.

It's an interesting reflection upon our consumer-driven society: one part propagates spending and the indulgence of immediate desires, while the other preaches restraint, foresight, and prudent financial management. The overlap of these two societal messages creates a complex tapestry where individuals must navigate their financial journey, cautiously deciphering which messages align with their fiscal health and long-term financial stability.

The intertwined relationship between pop culture, media portrayal of debt, and individual financial management evolves into a discussion that branches into numerous aspects of daily life, societal expectations, and personal wellbeing. How does one insulate themselves from the pervasive messages that encourage, either overtly or covertly, a lifestyle potentially financed by debt? It invariably involves a personal journey of understanding, a structured approach to financial management, and perhaps, a recalibration of values and aspirations that resist the omnipresent societal messages that so often lure individuals into a cycle of perpetual debt and financial instability.

The navigation through a culture steeped in the glamorization of debt necessitates a steadfast awareness and a structured approach to personal finance. This not only entails resisting the prevalent messages which permeate through various media but also fostering a robust, personalized financial strategy that provides a buffer against the ceaseless bombardment of encouragement to indulge in a lifestyle that may not align with one's financial reality. This, in itself, becomes an act of subtle rebellion against the ingrained narratives embedded within our society, offering a pathway to financial wellness that transcends the appealing yet potentially hazardous messages of unrestrained consumerism.

How educational systems fail to address financial literacy

Debt is an omnipresent aspect of modern society, influencing myriad lives in varied and complex ways. The notion of owing money, be it to financial institutions or individuals, evokes various emotions and judgments from different sections of society. There is a pronounced divide in perspectives when it comes to understanding why people find themselves buried under the weight of financial obligations. While some may perceive it as a result of unavoidable circumstances, others may attribute it to negligence or mismanagement of finances. This spectrum of judgments and misconceptions regarding those in debt often stems from a limited understanding of the person's individual journey, the socio-economic factors impacting them, and, importantly, the educational framework that has guided their financial literacy.

My story reflects a struggle that intertwines with this very issue - the insufficiency of financial literacy education within the schooling system and its subsequent impact on understanding and managing debt. From a personal standpoint, financial literacy is quintessential, not just as a skill but as a lifeline to navigate the financial labyrinth that life often becomes. School, a place where varied life skills are taught, startlingly fell short when it came to imparting knowledge about managing finances, doing taxes, budgeting, or understanding the implications of debt. My sole encounter with a lesson about personal finance transpired in an economics class during my senior year of high school, where our understandings of saving and spending were superficially explored.

When asked about our future financial plans, most of my classmates exhibited a conservative approach, favoring saving a significant chunk of their income over spending. My perspective diverged notably - I envisioned saving only 20% of my income, allocating the rest to spending. This viewpoint was not derived from a place of recklessness, but rather was deeply rooted in my upbringing and experiences. Despite the apparent financial hardships my family navigated through - foreclosures, reliance on food stamps, perpetual working hours, and a health crisis - there was a cycle of working hard and rewarding that hard work with spending, which I observed keenly. My parents, continually battered by the rigorous tides of maintaining financial stability, found ephemeral solace in spending, providing a brief respite from the tirelessness of their daily grind. A cycle I unknowingly adopted and carried forward into my adulthood, albeit with my own nuances.

The years that followed revealed the pitfalls of this cycle. Despite earning a substantial income in a stable 8-5 job, I found myself ensnared in debt, partly a result of habits formed without a proper educational foundation in financial management. My desire for the luxuries and extravagances that were inaccessible during my childhood propelled my spending, diminishing the part of my income that could have been efficiently saved or invested. This reflection isn't about lamenting the lack of restraint but understanding that my educational journey did little to equip me with the skills necessary to manage my finances astutely.

The first brush with the complexity of managing large sums of money and understanding debt came with my first student loan. Unsurprisingly, the education system did nothing to elucidate the intricacies of financial aid, loans, scholarships, and grants. This information, vital to making informed decisions about my future, was navigated with the assistance of my grandmother, sitting on her family room floor, figuring out what the numbers meant and how they would impact my life post-graduation. My naivety and the absence of a proper understanding of the financial burden I was assuming lead me to underestimate the implications of a 40K debt, thinking it would be easily managed once I stepped into the working world.

A gross miscalculation, as it turned out. Post-graduation life brought with it not just the pressures of paying back the loan but also managing rent, bills, food, and numerous other necessities that constituted adult life. Despite having a stable income, the spectral presence of debt lingered perpetually in my existence, a constant reminder of the financial literacy skills I lacked, which the education system failed to provide. Ironically, it was Youtube, not school, that became my teacher in the arena of personal finance. Various content creators shared wisdom regarding wealth building, money management, and spending practices, which I amalgamated to formulate a strategy suitable to my circumstances.

The importance of incorporating personal finance into the high school curriculum, at least to some degree, cannot be overstressed. The absence of this critical education, coupled with the mixed financial messages from my family, made the path to financial literacy an uphill battle. While my grandmother was a beacon of wisdom in this aspect, the lack of formal, widespread education on the topic exposes countless individuals to the stresses and challenges of debt management without providing them with the necessary tools to navigate through it.

The conceptualization of debt often fails to consider the structural inadequacies that people encounter in their journey through financial management. When society perceives those in debt, it's crucial to understand the backdrop against which such situations arise. It's not merely about recklessness or intentional mismanagement, but often a lack of knowledge, resources, and sometimes, a safety net to fall back on. An inclusive perspective towards understanding the various factors that contribute to an individual's financial situation is essential. Judgments and misconceptions only serve to further isolate and stigmatize individuals who are potentially grappling with the harsh realities of their financial circumstances, without offering constructive solutions or support to navigate out of it. It's pivotal to shift the lens through which we view debt and those navigating it, transitioning from a place of judgment to one of understanding and empathy. This not only mitigates the societal pressure experienced by those in debt but also facilitates a healthier dialogue about managing and overcoming financial challenges.

The normalization of debt in society

Debt has become a staple in the contemporary socio-economic landscape, veering away from being a mere financial tool to an inevitable part of life for many. This has been influenced and exacerbated by numerous factors, such as increasing living costs, stagnating wages, and the pervasive marketing of the consumerist lifestyle. This normalization of debt threads through society, affecting financial behaviors, lifestyles, and even our mental well-being, bridging the gap between what we earn and what we desire to consume. The ease and accessibility of acquiring debt have positioned it as a feasible solution for immediate financial hurdles or aspirations, thus embedding it deeply into our daily lives.

In the context of one's experiences, the educational aspect of managing finances and understanding debt often finds itself at the peripheral. Growing up with a notion that using debt to leverage opportunities, especially in aspects like education, can sometimes blur the lines between strategic financial planning and entrapping oneself in a vicious cycle. The idea that taking on debt for educational purposes will unequivocally lead to a brighter financial future is heavily marketed, yet the reality can be starkly different. The weight of student loans, for instance, doesn't merely rest on the shoulders as a financial burden, but transforms into a mental and emotional load, persistently nudging the trajectory of life decisions and career choices.

My personal journey echoes a similar narrative. My initial views on debt were primarily shaped by societal norms and familial experiences, where leveraging debt to generate future wealth, particularly through education, was widely accepted and encouraged. However, the profound reality hit hard as the debts piled up, morphing from a means to an end into a stifling obstacle, hindering my financial progression and seeding stress into my daily existence. My life unfolded amidst contrasting financial strategies employed by my grandparents and parents. While my grandma astutely utilized debt to accrue assets like real estate, my parents often navigated through consumer debts, subtly infusing in me a nuanced perspective of managing finances and liabilities. This bi-faceted exposure, though enlightening in ways, also left me teetering between financial prudence and imprudence, swaying between asset acquisition and yielding to consumeristic tendencies.

Experiencing firsthand the repercussions of significant financial commitments, I embarked on an inward journey, scrutinizing my debts, spending habits, and the emotional whirlwind entwined with them. Financial strain wasn't merely numerical; it bled into my psychological state, affecting my peace of mind and directing my life choices. The omnipresent commercials preaching the convenience of buy-now-pay-later plans and easy loan availabilities did little to abate my struggles; instead, they enticed me into further expenditures, perpetuating a cycle that negated financial stability. Encounters with such deceptive financial avenues underscored the profound disconnection between societal debt norms and financial well-being.

I've come across numerous videos detailing how repo companies are overwhelmed, unable to keep up with the surge of repossession orders. These narratives serve as a testament to the broader societal issue at hand. The seductive appeal of possessions, showcased through glossy advertising and made accessible by easy credit options, can lead individuals down a perilous financial path. Many get lured into the trap of securing hefty loans for luxury items like high-end cars, enticed by the dream rather than the practicality. They might be presented with unfavorable terms, but the thought of driving the car of their dreams overshadows the stark reality of potential future financial struggles. This facade paints a picture where owning ostentatious assets, even with exorbitant monthly payments, becomes normalized, often neglecting the underlying financial stability required. This perpetuates a toxic culture where financial literacy is overshadowed by a seemingly glamorous lifestyle, often achieved at the brink of crippling debt.

Navigating through this tumultuous journey of understanding and managing debt, I discovered the importance of not just being financially literate, but also of imparting this knowledge to subsequent generations. The resistance against the conventional debt culture and the resolve to chart a course towards financial stability has propelled me into advocating for financial literacy and prudence. This doesn't translate into a frugal lifestyle devoid of leisure and enjoyment but encourages a balanced approach where financial decisions are not driven by societal pressure or transient desires, but by sustainability and foresight.

It is quintessential to acknowledge the intricate relationship between societal norms, personal financial habits, and the psychological implications thereof. As witnessed through lived experiences, while debt can be a strategic tool for certain investments, like acquiring appreciating assets, it can also serve as a slippery slope towards financial instability when wielded imprudently for depreciating liabilities. Observing and learning from the generational approaches to debt, from asset acquisition to consumer spending, casts a reflective light upon the necessity to discern between beneficial and detrimental financial commitments. It beckons a thorough introspection and restructuring of our financial habits, enabling us to break free from the shackles of normalized debt culture, thereby steering towards a future that is not just financially secure but also mentally serene.

In the broader canvas, understanding and confronting the systemic normalization of debt implores an evaluation and reformation at both macro and micro levels of society. It demands an infusion of financial education into the foundational years of learning, ensuring future generations are equipped to navigate through the complex financial landscapes with informed discernment. Additionally, policy reforms and regulatory frameworks need to prioritize financial stability and protection for individuals, especially against exploitative lending practices that perpetuate the cycle of debt. Ultimately, while debt will likely continue to permeate our societies, its normalization need not predicate a pathway towards financial instability. With informed perspectives, pragmatic approaches, and structural support, individuals can steer their financial ships, strategically utilizing debt without being engulfed by it.

BREAKING FREE: STEPS TOWARDS A DEBT-FREE LIFE

Assessing and acknowledging the full scope of one's debt

Peering into the abyss of one's financial liabilities, truly seeing the vastness of debt, is an exercise in courage and sober acceptance. Acknowledging the full scope of debt necessitates a raw, unflinching confrontation with reality, often revealing the spiderweb of choices and habits that allowed the debt to burgeon in the first place. In a society where consumerism often steers the helm, where immediate gratification often overshadows fiscal responsibility, falling into the snare of debt becomes almost an unspoken norm. Debts, with their accumulating interests and varied terms, can silently and gradually weave a complex tapestry that, once illuminated, is overwhelming and oppressive to behold. And it's within this stark realization that the journey towards financial liberation usually commences.

I distinctly recall the moment when everything shifted, dramatically altering the trajectory of my financial life: my engagement. This was a moment that not only symbolized a union of hearts but also presented an acute, tangible obstacle, starkly framed against the backdrop of shared future aspirations. My formerly foggy, abstract conception of debt suddenly became a tangible, immediate threat, casting a looming shadow over my path towards matrimony.

My acknowledgment of this debt was more than just an analytical task; it became an emotionally laden recognition, a burden that was no longer peripheral but at the forefront, urgently demanding my attention and action. My physical reflection revealed more than just my external self; it unveiled the choices, an external semblance of an internal, fiscal tumult that had long been ignored. My weight gain and unhealthy living were merely symptoms of a larger issue: a disregard for the future consequences of present comforts and desires, permeating not just my eating habits, but also my spending behaviors.

The cascade of emotions when the realization dawned upon me about the gravity of dragging debt into our marital life was like a tidal wave of awakening, striking with both fear and clarity. My heart pulsed loudly in my ears, a rhythmic reminder of the responsibility and obligation I felt towards my fiancé, towards our collective future. Each figure in my debt summary was not just a number but a shackle, tethering our shared dreams to a stagnant reality, obstructing the unfurling of our wings to soar into our shared future. I visualized the stress lines on my future self, the apologetic glances towards my partner whenever financial topics arose, and the stifling weight that would hang between us, an unspoken strain sourced from unaddressed fiscal imprudence. My throat constricted at the mere thought of her ever having to shoulder my past indiscretions and choices. It became more than a self-promise; it morphed into a solemn vow that her life, our life, would not be tainted by the ghost of my financial past.

Immersed in a cocktail of determination mixed with sporadic bursts of anxiety, my approach to money, spending, and debt transformed into a carefully choreographed dance between necessity and desire. Each potential expenditure became a battleground, where the warriors of immediate satisfaction clashed with the soldiers of financial stability and future planning. It was no longer just about me, my wants, or even my needs. It became a symphony where every note played impacted not only my present but resonated through the future corridors of our life together. Each moment of saying "no" to a want was a moment of saying "yes" to a future unburdened by past financial mistakes.

The creation and adherence to a budget, the sidelining of wants and immediate desires, all became part of a new, stringent reality. Every penny was scrutinized, every expenditure challenged, every financial decision was weighed against the overarching goal of debt eradication. Conversations around finances, once vague and uncomfortable, became frequent, honest, and essential. Transparent, genuine exchanges became a vital component of my new, fiscally responsible reality.

The relentless discipline to eradicate debt ahead of our union, to enter this new chapter unburdened, meant consistently navigating through a consumer-driven society, pulsating with temptations and perpetual offerings of immediate pleasure. Debts were no longer just numbers; they represented deferred dreams, postponed milestones, and potential familial burdens.

Even something as seemingly trivial as contemplating a video game purchase became a complex calculus of values and priorities. I stared at the colorful cover, absorbed by a world of an alternate virtual reality, a temporary escape from the sobering facts of my own reality. But then, a flood of images and thoughts besieged my mind: images of my fiancée, our dreams of a home together, and an unspoken promise of shared prosperity. The $60 price tag, once so easily justified, now seemed insurmountable, no longer merely a numerical value but a symbolic choice between transient pleasure and long-term collective happiness. Each pixel of enjoyment the game promised became a pixel of a future jeopardized, a potential step back on my journey to financial well-being. My fingers lingered over the 'purchase' button, teetering on the brink, the old me battling with the new, resolved me. It was a moment that transcended beyond a simple purchase decision, becoming a poignant metaphor of my changed financial perspective: where every expenditure, regardless of its size, was scrutinized against the backdrop of a future built on financial stability and freedom.

Throughout this tumultuous journey, which soared through peaks of financial revelation and dove into valleys of stark self-reflection, a path was carved. A path that was as much about unburdening my future self and loved ones as it was about reconciling with my past choices and forging a new identity, not tethered to debt, but liberated from it.

In recognizing and addressing my debt, I experienced an intertwining of financial recalibrations with emotional reckonings, resulting in a journey that demanded the abandonment of entrenched habits, the adoption of stringent disciplines, and most pivotally, the resilience to sustain momentum even when faced with steep challenges. It is a story that intricately ties fiscal prudence with emotional intelligence, providing not just a cautionary tale, but hopefully, inspiring the courage within others to commence their own journeys towards financial freedom.

Peering beyond the digits and the budgets, this journey uncovered an essential human experience of confronting one's weaknesses yet finding the fortitude to alter the course towards a place of freedom, stability, and self-assurance. It is a trek that many undertake, each journey inherently personal and distinct, weaving its own story of struggle, enlightenment, and eventual tranquility in financial stability. The expanse of debts and financial obligations tells a story of resilience and learning, scripting a narrative of liberation that is as liberating as it is enlightening.

Prioritizing and strategizing repayments

Understanding the complexity and struggle inherent in debt management can unveil a journey wrought with emotional turmoil and steadfast resolve. The endeavor of prioritizing and strategizing repayments is critical in orchestrating a pathway out of the financial abyss, especially when one is entangled in various types of debts. It's not merely about throwing money at what you owe; it's a calculated, and often emotionally taxing, strategy that requires scrutinizing interest rates, understanding payment terms, and ensuring that the chosen path not only alleviates debt but is also sustainable in the long term without escalating financial stress.

Embarking on a journey through the intricate and sometimes chaotic realm of debt management, I found myself encapsulated in a whirlwind of emotional peaks and valleys. Wrestling with the strategy of prioritizing and strategizing repayments, my narrative weaves through various chapters, each possessing its own financial ethos and emotional resonance.

I will breakdown my uncomplex complex strategy of repaying my debts in two part, pre and post engagement. In the backdrop of my pre-engagement era, I now perceive a version of myself somewhat nonchalant and arguably cavalier in my approach toward debt. Here I was, a fresh graduate, saddled with various debts ranging from student loans to credit card fluctuations and eventually, a motorcycle loan. recall with a certain fondness yet underscored by a subtle pang of regret how I managed my student loans, which were, at the start, quite a hefty sum of 40K. It wasn't merely a number. It was a mountain, one that shadowed over the early years of my professional life.

The breakdown of the student loan was somewhat like this: 13K with a provider labeled UAS and 27K tethered to Nelnet. Intriguingly, I distinctly remember initiating an auto-debit system for my loans, which at face value, seemed like a reasonably responsible move. Upon receiving my salary, $125 was systematically siphoned off each week – $50 cascading into UAS and $75 funneling into Nelnet. The minimum monthly requirement for Nelnet loomed at around $280, and while I can't quite recall the exact figures for UAS, I know it nestled below $200.

At that time, this system of automated payments felt like a prudent strategy. The concept was straightforward: ensure that the loan was being addressed, eliminate the risk of late payments, and, theoretically, allow myself to carve out a financial life beyond the shadow of my educational debt. My loans were, after all, being serviced without a second thought, providing me a semblance of financial autonomy and erasing the need to consciously engage with the weight of my debt.

Yet, the present-day me beholds this strategy with discerning eyes, recognizing the missed opportunities that lingered in the background of this automated system. Although my debts were being addressed, they were not being engaged with. My payment strategy, in its automated simplicity, failed to explore potential optimizations, nor did it consider accelerating the repayment to liberate future me from the financial shackles sooner.

Reflecting on it now, I realize that while the strategy of consistent, automated payments safeguarded my credit score and slowly chipped away at the principal, it perhaps also fostered a degree of financial complacency. My money was working, but it wasn't working hard. My strategy was functional but not optimal, ensuring steady progression towards debt elimination but not facilitating an accelerated journey towards financial liberation.

I muse now over what could have been if the fervor and financial diligence that characterizes my current self were present during those initial post-collegiate years. Would I have scrutinized my expenditures with more intensity, perhaps funneling additional resources towards my loans to expedite their demise? Could I have engaged in a more aggressive repayment strategy, liberating my future self from the financial burden that much sooner?

Navigating through that chapter, I see not just financial decisions but emotional journeys where each expenditure, whether rational or impulsive, told a story of youthful exuberance and perhaps, ignorance. Engaging in a delicate ballet of managing multiple financial obligations while indulging in a somewhat hedonistic approach towards expenditure, I was often blind to the snowballing future implications of my financial decisions.

However, something pivotal happened post-engagement, a cataclysmic shift both in financial circumstance and emotional resonance towards debt. Suddenly, the somewhat distant echo of financial accountability became a deafening roar, propelling me into a newfound reality where the debt was not just figures on a screen, but a palpable, oppressive entity. Engulfed by over 20K in credit card debt and still 24 left in student loans, I found myself at a financial crossroads, where I was coerced to confront the consequences of past decisions while navigating a pathway towards a stable financial future.

In this second epoch, I delved into an intricate dance with my finances, methodically chipping away at high-interest debts while immersing myself in a world of financial education and discipline that was previously alien to me. Budgeting, once perceived as a financial straitjacket, transformed into an invaluable ally, illuminating the recesses of my financial landscape and enabling a strategic and informed approach towards debt elimination. I witnessed the fading of financial vagueness and the crystallization of a clear, albeit challenging, path forward.

As I submerged myself into the realms of financial influencers like The Dave Ramsey Show, Caleb Hammer and Graham Stephan, absorbing invaluable nuggets of financial wisdom, I sculpted a more structured, deliberate approach towards expenditure and debt repayment. I meticulously itemized my expenses, ensuring each dollar was assigned a 'job' and optimizing extra funds to accelerate my journey out of debt.

In this reflective contemplation, I realize that prioritizing and strategizing repayments were far more than numerical gymnastics – it was an emotional and psychological metamorphosis. My evolution from the uninhibited spender of my pre-engagement days to a disciplined, financially conscious individual post-engagement is not merely a tale of financial reformation. It's a story of awakening, realization, and a stubborn, unyielding resolve to sever the chains of debt and bask in the liberating glory of financial freedom.

Navigating through the final throes of my debt-laden journey, I understood that this was not just about erasing figures from a balance sheet. It was about reconstructing my relationship with money, reshaping my financial destiny, and ensuring that the fiscal sins of the past did not dictate the chapters of my future.

I now stand on the precipice of the future, gazing into a horizon where my income is not pillaged by the ghosts of past expenditures. It's a future where financial decisions are sculpted by dreams, aspirations, and deliberate choice, not by the oppressive weight of outstanding obligations.

In extrapolating my journey, I convey not just a strategy but a testament to the transformative power of financial education, discipline, and a steadfast resolve to navigate towards fiscal autonomy. A part of this journey has involved setting clear financial milestones: establishing a $1,000 emergency savings fund (a goal I've proudly achieved), aggressively tackling high-interest debt (a mission nearly completed), and setting sights on bolstering my emergency fund to a range of $3,000 to $5,000 (the next step on my path). After establishing this safety net, my primary focus will shift to clearing my low-interest student loans, which currently stand at $24K. While making the monthly minimum payments, establishing a solid financial foundation remains paramount. Through the lens of my own missteps, triumphs, and ongoing journey, I hope to illuminate a pathway for others teetering on the brink of financial despair, providing not just a roadmap but a beacon of hope that even amidst the tempest of debt, the shores of financial peace are within reach.

This is my odyssey through the realm of debt – a tapestry interwoven with financial strategies, emotional tumult, and an unwavering resolve to forge ahead, even when the path seemed insurmountably steep. This narrative is not merely figures and strategies; it's a deeply personal journey through the emotional and psychological landscapes of debt management, underscoring that beyond every financial decision lies an emotional subtext, a story of struggle, triumph, and perpetual evolution towards financial enlightenment and freedom.

Budgeting and living within means

Navigating through the winding roads of financial discipline, budgeting stands out as a quintessential practice that's often easier said than done. The theoretical simplicity of aligning expenses with income masks the intricate dynamics and emotional undercurrents of ensuring each dollar is intentionally spent. Budgeting isn't merely a financial activity; it's a reflective process, an ongoing dialogue with oneself about priorities, desires, necessities, and the continual balancing act that stitches them all together. It is about orchestrating a lifestyle that finds harmony in current enjoyments and future freedoms, threading the needle between immediate gratifications and long-term wellbeing.

My own venture into budgeting did not originate from a deeply rooted understanding of its importance, but rather from a necessity instilled by past lapses in financial judgement. For a large portion of my life, my financial planning was, at best, superficial. Everything was straightforward: automated payments took care of my debts and necessary expenses, and whatever remained was mine to expend as I pleased. No restrictions, no second thoughts, and certainly no forward-looking financial strategy. The semblance of managing my finances was essentially an auto debit setup for my credit card and loans, and an arbitrary, unstructured spending plan for what remained.

However, when I found myself seriously sitting down and drafting a budget for the first time, it wasn't merely a task; it was an awakening. Utilizing Google Sheets, primarily for its cost-effectiveness, I sculpted an evolving budget that transformed with every pay period. The process was not just about predicting and controlling my spending, but rather it created a space where I could visualize my financial journey, understanding the pathway each dollar took from my paycheck to its final destination. Because my current living situation allowed me to save on rent, living with future in-laws, my initial budget was primarily targeted towards addressing my debts, while allocating funds for essentials such as gas, food, and incidental expenses, with a tentative cap of 500 dollars every two weeks for necessities.

Wants and needs, two simple words yet, in practice, their differentiation became a profound learning curve. I wanted to obliterate my debt, a goal that nudged me towards evaluating my spending with a discerning eye. By setting a spending threshold, I was able to streamline my financial focus, ensuring that a significant chunk of my income was funneled towards debt repayment as soon as it entered my account, while the allocated budget ensured I remained financially stable for the fortnight. The fiscal self-discipline I began to cultivate didn't stem from a restrictive mindset, but rather from a conscious acknowledgment of my future aspirations and current realities.

It wasn't always a smooth sail, especially when it came to dismantling the habits that were deeply ingrained in my everyday life. For instance, the convenience of ordering food through apps like GrubHub and Postmates was a notorious money-drain. The easy, one-click access to meals became a vortex of continuous spending, where one lazy decision spurred another, propelling me further away from my financial goals. The decision to delete these apps, thus forcing myself into the kitchen, wasn't just a budgeting choice. It was a reclamation of control, not just over my spending, but over my daily choices, routines, and ultimately, my life.

Travel, another financial behemoth, still poses a challenge. My love for exploring new places, savoring exotic foods, and immersing myself in diverse cultures has always stood at odds with my budgeting goals. While currently in a hiatus due to my relocation to LA and the ensuing settling-in period, I am determined that my future travels will be characterized by thorough budgeting. The plan? To allocate funds even for unexpected experiences, ensuring that spontaneity doesn't translate into financial turbulence, and every adventure is savored without a subsequent financial hangover.

Social pressures and temptations, often the silent sabotagers of a well-intended budget, surprisingly, became aspects I managed to navigate with relative ease. Perhaps, it was my newfound financial clarity and the confidence to communicate about my financial journey that allowed me to erect a resilient barrier against societal spending pressures. The insight gained through my journey instilled a steadfastness that empowered me to say 'no' without a shadow of guilt or fear of missing out. My allowances for hobbies, like video games and tech gadgets, are conscientiously enveloped within a specific range, ensuring that my pursuits for leisure and enjoyment are not entirely stifled by my budgeting practices.

Ensuring that my budget remains adhered to, especially when it pertains to allocating every possible dollar towards my debts, has been a journey of its own. Every paycheck is dissected, budgeted, and the excess instantly channeled towards debt repayment. This almost mechanical methodology, while highly effective in its current state, also births a realization: once the debts are cleared, a new approach, a fresh perspective on handling 'excess' money will be imperative, to ensure that it is not lost to the abyss of unchecked spending.

Resonating forward, budgeting has become more than a tool; it has evolved into a mindset. A perspective that acknowledges the financial ebbs and flows of life, respects the scarcity of resources, and appreciates the beauty of achieving a goal through disciplined action and intentional decision-making. It has become a dialogue, where my past self, replete with financial missteps and impulsive decisions, converses with my present self, creating a narrative that doesn't just recount a story of transformation but serves as a continuous reminder that every financial decision, big or small, is a stitch in the fabric of my financial future.

Budgeting isn't merely about numbers; it's also about perceptions, emotions, and the subtle yet profound relationship we have with our resources. It is an ongoing journey where every recalibration, every decision, and every sacrifice or indulgence shapes the path forward. The liberation from debt isn't just about breaking free from financial chains, but also about reshaping the very relationship one has with money, embedding it not with fear or resentment, but with respect, understanding, and intentional stewardship. And so, the journey towards a debt-free life meanders, not just through the tangible realms of income, expenses, and debts but through the introspective paths of desires, disciplines, and dreams.

Seeking professional help: financial advisors, therapists, etc.

Embarking on a journey toward financial stability, particularly when enshrouded by the looming shadow of debt, undoubtedly requires more than unbridled determination and a rudimentary plan. The challenge of maneuvering through debt, coordinating various financial responsibilities, and safeguarding mental well-being throughout this demanding journey innately calls for professional involvement. Financial advisors, therapists, and possibly legal consultants become instrumental, guiding through the tumultuous seas of debt management while also acting as sentinels of mental tranquility during this complex period. With my own personal endeavors and struggles through debt, I've come to a reflective decision: once I successfully navigate through my existing financial obligations and amass a lump sum, engaging a financial advisor will likely be my next prudent step to fortifying and augmenting my fiscal stability and future security. This decision is not just about wealth management but also about ensuring continued financial education and stability, preventing past mishaps from recurring in future chapters of my financial story.

The initial step in welcoming professional help is recognizing its imperative nature. The labyrinthine world of debt, with its numerous options, routes, and potential pitfalls, can be overwhelmingly intricate for an individual to navigate alone. It is essential to understand that seeking help is neither a sign of weakness nor an indication of incompetency. Instead, it is a prudent acknowledgment that certain areas of our lives, especially those as crucial and complex as financial management, often demand expert guidance.

Understanding the intricacies of financial management can be a complex and daunting task, especially when juggling debts across various platforms. A financial advisor brings expertise to the table, illuminating viable paths, demystifying complex financial terminologies and instruments, and ultimately assisting in creating a viable plan tailored to an individual's unique financial situation. People might seek a financial advisor to gain clarity, ensure their approach is strategic and optimized, and to navigate through the complexities of financial planning and debt management with a knowledgeable ally by their side.

The pros of engaging a financial advisor are manifold. Firstly, they provide expert insights and guide individuals towards making informed decisions, thereby potentially preventing costly mistakes. They assist in formulating a structured financial plan, which is essential to track and manage income, expenses, savings, and debt repayment strategically. Furthermore, financial advisors can act as accountability partners, ensuring that individuals remain committed to their financial plans and goals. Their knowledge also extends to understanding various financial instruments and strategies that might be utilized to optimize wealth creation and debt management, thereby potentially accelerating the journey towards financial freedom.

While I am not a financial advisor or qualified to even give financial advice, I'd encourage those curious about personal finance to delve into YouTube videos on the topic. Numerous creators break down their paychecks, showcasing their budgeting methods and strategies. The internet is teeming with knowledge on this front, and viewing various perspectives can offer a comprehensive understanding, helping you craft a unique strategy tailored to your circumstances.

On the emotional front, having a financial advisor can provide a psychological respite. Knowing that a knowledgeable professional is steering your financial ship can alleviate anxiety related to money management and debt. It fosters a sense of security, knowing that the devised strategies and approaches are backed by expert knowledge and tailored to your unique financial context.

However, engaging a financial advisor is not without its cons. One of the most glaring drawbacks is the cost associated with hiring a professional advisor. Especially when an individual is already saddled with debt, the additional financial burden of professional fees might seem counterintuitive. Furthermore, the benefits of a financial advisor are heavily contingent upon the expertise and proficiency of the advisor. An incompetent or unsuitable advisor might not only fail to optimize your financial situation but could potentially exacerbate it. Therefore, the process of selecting an appropriate advisor, who not only brings expertise but also understands and respects your financial philosophy and objectives, is crucial and can be challenging.

Moreover, a financial advisor would need comprehensive access to your financial details to formulate effective strategies. For some, divulging such intimate details can be uncomfortable or anxiety-inducing. It's essential that a solid foundation of trust is established, and ensuring this whilst managing the vulnerability that comes with exposing financial scars can be a delicate process.

Additionally, while financial advisors bring valuable expertise, there is no guarantee of success or profitability from the formulated strategies. The financial markets are influenced by a plethora of factors and are inherently risky and unpredictable to various degrees. Consequently, even with expert advice, investments can underperform, and financial strategies might not yield the anticipated results.

While financial advisors can provide pivotal guidance, support, and strategic input, it is vital to weigh the potential benefits against the inherent costs and risks. This involves considering not only the tangible costs and benefits but also personal comfort, trust, and the psychological impact of exposing and sharing financial woes and missteps. Regardless, in many scenarios, especially when dealing with complex financial instruments, significant debt, or when feeling overwhelmed by financial decisions, a financial advisor can be an invaluable ally in navigating towards financial stability and freedom.

Upon deciding to engage with a financial advisor, the first agenda typically involves developing a robust financial plan. This encapsulates a detailed understanding of your current financial standing, future objectives, risk appetite, and any specific preferences or constraints you might have. The advisor then synthesizes this information, formulating a strategic plan that meticulously details your budgeting, savings, and debt repayment tactics, ensuring a cohesive approach towards your financial stability and freedom.

Parallelly, managing the emotional and psychological impact of debt is paramount. The persistent stress, potential anxiety, and occasionally the sinking feeling of despair associated with debt can be crippling. A therapist plays a crucial role in ensuring that you traverse through this journey with not just financial but also emotional stability. They provide the requisite support, strategies, and coping mechanisms, ensuring that while you tackle your debt, your mental well-being is not compromised.

Embarking on therapy, especially in the context of debt, involves more than merely venting frustrations or concerns. It entails forming a therapeutic alliance wherein the therapist assists you in recognizing patterns, triggers, and potential unhealthy coping mechanisms related to financial stress. They aid in developing healthier, more constructive strategies to manage stress and navigate through the emotional upheaval that debt can often stir. Moreover, they provide a safe, non-judgmental space where you can explore and address any deeper, perhaps hidden, emotional or psychological issues related to money and debt.

In instances where debt transcends mere financial management and permeates into legal territories, such as being summoned to court, dealing with insolvencies, or considering bankruptcy, legal advisors become indispensable. Their expertise in legal statutes, rights, and regulations pertinent to debt ensures that you are not only protected legally but are also making informed decisions that won't inadvertently jeopardize your financial future.

Before considering the engagement of a financial advisor, it's paramount to first have a baseline understanding of your own finances. Familiarize yourself with your income streams, monthly expenses, existing debts, and savings. This foundational grasp will not only facilitate a productive dialogue with any professional but also empower you in your financial journey.

One of the potential hurdles or objections toward hiring professionals relates to their cost. When mired in debt, the thought of incurring additional expenses can be daunting. However, it is imperative to conduct a nuanced cost-benefit analysis, considering not just the immediate financial outlay but also the long-term financial, emotional, and psychological benefits. Moreover, one should weigh the potential costs of not seeking help, as sometimes, expert guidance can prevent far greater financial pitfalls in the future.

Celebrating small victories on the road to being debt-free

Embracing the journey towards a debt-free life, particularly when entwined with layers of financial obligations and commitments, unfolds a path that is as much psychological as it is financial. Recognizing and celebrating the small victories along this path doesn't merely account for financial progress but serves as a fundamental element in maintaining emotional and psychological well-being. The modest advancements, like making a timely payment, avoiding new debts, or even sticking rigorously to a budget, reflect minute yet critical triumphs that incrementally build towards the ultimate goal of financial liberation. However, acknowledging these achievements is not just about ticking boxes on a financial checklist but embodying a methodology that intertwines fiscal responsibility with emotional acknowledgment and reward.

Navigating through the strenuous pathway to becoming debt-free, my own experiences have starkly highlighted the pivotal role that acknowledging and celebrating small victories plays. The undulating journey, inherently rife with both struggles and successes, is as emotionally draining as it is financially challenging. Each pay period, watching the debt balance trickle downwards, while certainly a relief, also unveils its own set of emotional and psychological challenges. Employing an app like Mint not only assisted me in tracking my net worth and observing it gradually inflate as my debts deflated, but it also presented a semblance of light, a numeric affirmation that each step, no matter how small, was a step forward.

Indeed, witnessing a debt account flicker to zero was at times a complex emotional experience, encapsulating relief, achievement, and also a peculiar emptiness. To ensure that each such victory was acknowledged and celebrated, while also safeguarding against financial indulgence, my rewards were meticulously planned and always aligned with my overarching financial strategy. Rewinding into the worlds of cherished old games or delving into new anime episodes within an already-budgeted subscription were modes of celebration that neither derailed my financial plan nor diminished the value of the victory.

Celebration, for me, was never synonymous with financial extravagance. Rather, it was about acknowledging progress, taking a moment to breathe, and allowing myself a reprieve within predefined financial boundaries. It was vital for my mental state to ensure that the financial control I was gradually reclaiming was not stifled by the paradox of financially imprudent celebrations. Each small win, each dollar saved, and each debt account closed, reflected not merely a numeric progression but an evolution in my financial mindset and control. It was about transforming the narrative from being controlled by my debts to being in control of them.

With time, as debts were consistently addressed and slowly eradicated, my approach to money and spending organically transformed. Rewards no longer needed to be tangible or financial. Simply observing my progress, setting, and then achieving new financial goals, and even periodically allowing myself the financial breathing space to enjoy a little budgeted entertainment, became celebrations in themselves. They symbolized not only the tangible progress being made but also a consistent adherence to a philosophy of financial responsibility and autonomy.

My vision for a future unburdened by debt, where choices can be made freely and without the omnipresent shadow of financial obligations, played a substantial role in fueling my journey. Even the smallest milestones were significant, not just as isolated achievements but as stepping stones towards a future of financial freedom and stability. I learned to prioritize, to plan, and to strategize, ensuring that every financial decision was made consciously, with both immediate and future implications considered.

Relationships, too, played a critical role in my journey. Ensuring transparency with my fiancée regarding my finances, objectives, and budget was not merely about maintaining an open line of communication but about creating a supportive and understanding environment within which my debt-free journey could unfold. Her support, positivity, and willingness to align with and support my financial goals and strategies significantly impacted my ability to stay the course, ensuring that the path, while often challenging, was never trodden alone.

The mindset that each debt paid off was a step closer to entering our marriage unburdened by past financial choices was a potent motivator. It was more than merely a desire to be debt-free; it was about ensuring that the union we were building was founded upon a stable, secure financial base. It was about ensuring that our future decisions, whether financial or otherwise, were made freely and without being constrained or influenced by past debts.

Navigating the path towards a debt-free existence is as much about managing finances as it is about managing emotions, relationships, and psychological well-being. Celebrating small victories not only serves to acknowledge the progress being made but also to reinforce the mindset, habits, and strategies that have facilitated this progress. It is about ensuring that the journey, while often challenging, also includes moments of reflection, acknowledgment, and celebration. These moments not only honor the progress that has been made but also serve to mentally and emotionally fortify against the challenges that yet lie ahead. Ultimately, each small victory celebrated is a step closer to not merely a debt-free life but a future where financial decisions can be made autonomously, strategically, and without the weighty shackles of past debts influencing the path forward.

PREVENTION: BUILDING A DEBT-RESISTANT FUTURE

Taking the first step

Taking charge of your personal finances is a profound journey of discovery, understanding, and eventual transformation. For many, the journey starts with a catalyst - a life-altering moment that forces them to take a hard look at their financial habits and the life they've built around them. For me, that moment arrived with the prospect of lifelong commitment, the moment I got engaged.

Until then, I had a nagging thought at the back of my mind about clearing my debt before I tied the knot. I envisioned a future where financial burdens were non-existent, and every new chapter of our life would commence on a clean slate. But as the years rolled by and our 8th anniversary approached, I found myself still grappling with debt. The weight of this realization was overwhelming. The idea of merging my life with someone, bringing with it the baggage of my financial mismanagement, was an alarming wake-up call. This wasn't just about me anymore; it was about us. The impending marriage underscored a responsibility not just to be a caring and loving partner, but also a financially responsible one. I couldn't bear the thought of my debt becoming a burden for her. This pivotal moment marked the start of my journey into the realm of personal finance with a renewed sense of purpose and diligence.

In hindsight, the financial decisions of my younger days seem mired in a phenomenon I now recognize as "lifestyle creep". With every pay raise, instead of saving or investing wisely, I found new avenues to spend. My expenses rose in tandem with my income. This spiral continued unchecked, and while I recognized it, I was ensnared in its loop, doing little to rectify it.

Emotions and money are deeply intertwined, and recognizing this is essential. When I was younger, financial decisions were driven by the pursuit of joy—buying things that made me happy in the moment, often without pondering their long-term value or impact. As debts mounted, that joy was quickly overshadowed by a looming sense of dread. The transition from the uninhibited joy of spending to the sobering reality of managing debt was a stark one.

The day I sat down to calculate my net worth was an eye-opener. On the surface, it seemed like I was doing things right. I was contributing to my retirement fund, ensuring that a chunk of my paycheck was invested even before it reached me. But when I factored in my debts, the picture that emerged was less rosy. It wasn't just about the numbers. It was a reflection of my choices, my priorities, and in many ways, the life I had crafted.

My meticulous foray into budgeting unearthed a myriad of insights. I unearthed unused subscriptions that were silently draining my account, extravagant spending on dining out, and a hefty sum allocated to travel. Every expense told a story, revealing not just my spending habits but also my values, desires, and sometimes, my lack of foresight.

Opening up about money is never easy. But as I began this new phase, I realized the power of dialogue. Discussing finances, be it triumphs, challenges, or aspirations, with trusted confidants was not just therapeutic but also educational. It provided a perspective outside of my own, sometimes offering solutions I hadn't considered.

Embarking on this new financial path, the challenges were numerous, but the clarity and peace of mind it brought were unparalleled. Taking that first step, embracing vulnerability, and facing financial realities head-on wasn't just about monetary stability. It was a promise to myself and to my future partner, a commitment to build a future not just on love and understanding, but also on financial trust and security.

In many ways, the world of personal finance is like a vast ocean. You can either stay on the shore, watching the waves and wondering what lies beyond, or you can take the plunge, navigating the depths, and discover treasures of wisdom and peace. The choice was mine to make, and I chose the latter. It required confronting some hard truths and making tougher choices, but every step, every decision, was a move towards a better future. The journey, while daunting at times, has been worth every sacrifice, every lesson learned. And as I continue to navigate the tumultuous seas of personal finance, I do so with the knowledge that every choice, every sacrifice, brings me closer to the future I aspire to, for myself and for my loved ones.

Instilling financial literacy in the next generation from a young age

Instilling financial literacy in the next generation from a young age is not merely an educational imperative; it's a collective responsibility that we, both you and I, shoulder. By prioritizing this, we're investing in a future where our children, nephews, nieces, or any young ones we influence, are equipped with the tools to make sound financial decisions. This early education plays a crucial role in ensuring that children grow with a mindful approach towards managing their resources and avoiding financial pitfalls, such as debt, that can become burdensome later in life. A foundational step in fostering a fiscally responsible future is to create a culture where children aren't just passively educated about money. Instead, they should actively witness, participate in, and engage with healthy financial practices and discussions within their homes and communities. In doing so, we lay the groundwork for a generation that not only understands the value of a dollar but also appreciates the broader implications of financial stewardship. It's upon us to lead by example and ensure that the legacy we leave behind is one of financial wisdom and prudence.

My earliest memory of handling money involves a blend of impulsiveness and caution. Whenever I got money from my parents or grandmother as a child, my immediate inclination was to buy something – toys, Pokémon cards, candy, whatever caught my fancy at the moment. But my true financial awakening, interestingly, occurred in high school when I got my first credit card, way before I even got a job. The card was meant for necessities like gas, and I had a modest limit of maybe $1,000. The weight of responsibility that came with it was palpable because I knew well not to mess around with the money – my grandmother, who backed it, would have not tolerated any mismanagement. Her insistence on responsible credit card usage, especially at a young age, greatly emphasized the importance of maintaining good credit.

My grandmother's strong advocacy for good credit stemmed from her own success that was facilitated by her ability to access low-interest rates and acquire properties. She was, and still is, a fervent heckler for maintaining a good credit score, firmly associating it with opportunities and financial stability. But my parents painted a starkly different picture. My mother, for instance, would frequently take me to the mall, spending hours shopping in her favorite stores like Forever 21. I was inadvertently absorbing consumerism in those endless hours, wandering through the mall, amidst plenty and extravagance, while she worked and shopped there.

It was during my college years that the restraints loosened, and I experienced all the financial freedom in the world. Initially, I exhibited reasonable financial behavior, judiciously using my credit card and ensuring it was paid off, primarily for the purpose of building credit. As my credit improved, my card's credit limit expanded, which unfortunately translated into an increased capacity to spend. My early financial blunders, particularly when my pay increased, were largely characterized by lifestyle inflation. More money equaled more spending. My financial missteps transitioned from shopping at Ross to shopping at Nordstrom, reflecting a marked change in my spending habits, even though I was a finance major – albeit not in Personal Finance.

Despite my degree, my understanding of money and its utilization didn't fully form until I consciously began thinking about my personal finances and ceased indiscriminate spending. My grandmother, through her firm and principled approach towards money, subconsciously instilled in me the ability to use money effectively, which has allowed me to better myself now that I am contemplating my personal finances more earnestly. Without her guidance and strict financial teachings, I would likely be floundering in a sea of debts and unnecessary expenditures today.

Tools and resources for managing finances during my younger years were quite limited. It essentially boiled down to my bank account – earning perhaps $120 a week and then watching it evaporate on food, gas, and occasionally, video games. There weren't too many tools available, but an underlying sense of money's responsibility lingered, gifted by my earlier experiences. If I were to devise a method or strategy to impart financial literacy to children, it would certainly encompass being transparent with them about personal finances, illustrating the cost of living, and explaining the balancing act of managing necessities, luxuries, and savings.

Speaking to children, when they reach an age of comprehension, about how life operates, how to raise and manage a family financially, and explaining why and how we afford things could provide them with a pragmatic view of money and its management. However, for those unfamiliar with sound personal finance practices themselves, who might struggle to guide their children in this domain, therein lies a significant challenge. This could be addressed, at least in part, by the education system taking a proactive role in teaching about personal finances, delineating the good from the bad in terms of loans and credit, and other fundamental financial knowledge.

Financial literacy is dynamic and constantly adapting to the shifting financial landscape and societal perceptions of money. Whereas credit was once touted for its convenience and ability to facilitate larger purchases, it has come under scrutiny for encouraging individuals to spend an additional 18% than if they were using cash. Similarly, while younger generations might perceive cash as an 'invisible currency' that allows them to make transactions without being tracked, they must also grasp the reality of its finite nature.

In today's rapidly evolving financial climate, it is imperative that we are agile, adapting and comprehending emerging trends and dialogues in the realm of personal finance. This enables us to engage in constructive discussions with younger generations, who might otherwise not comprehend money due to an environment where they may have experienced unbridled access to material wants. In doing so, we ensure that they are not only economically savvy but also capable of navigating the constantly shifting tides of the financial world with knowledge, competence, and a healthy respect for their fiscal resources.

Cultivating financial literacy from a young age will invariably contribute to the development of economically wise adults who can navigate their financial landscapes with competence and foresight. The amalgamation of practical financial education and healthy financial practices observed and discussed openly in familial and educational settings will pave the way for future generations to build and enjoy a stable, debt-resistant future. And as we guide the young ones along this path, we ensure not only their financial wellbeing but also the economic stability of societies at large.

The power of emergency funds and saving

Emergencies and unexpected financial burdens are inevitable aspects of life. An emergency fund and savings offer the financial buffer needed to manage these sudden expenditures without diving into a debt spiral. When adequately structured and responsibly maintained, these funds can not only handle unexpected costs but also provide a psychological cushion, offering peace of mind in knowing that one is prepared to address financial hiccups as they arise. This concept of creating a safety net emphasizes not just the practicality but also underscores a commitment towards a disciplined financial lifestyle.

Interestingly, for many, the path to understanding the crucial role of emergency funds often comes via personal experiences that underscore the tangible impacts of being caught unprepared in a financial crunch. For instance, my own journey towards understanding the power and necessity of an emergency fund wasn't straightforward. I hadn't really prioritized establishing an emergency fund until recently, as I embarked on a journey to revamp my personal finances. Conventional wisdom often cites starting with a $1,000 emergency fund, but in today's economic climate, especially here in 2023, emergencies can easily cost upwards of $3,000. While that initial $1,000 might seem insufficient, it does mark the commencement of a journey towards better financial management and personal development.

A pivotal moment that sharply underscored the value of having an emergency fund came unexpectedly one day when I awoke to excruciating tooth pain, arguably one of the most intense discomforts I've experienced - and I've had my fair share of painful episodes. From enduring stitches caused by a broken fence piercing my knee to surviving a skateboarding accident that scraped away half of my belly, leaving a scar that still lingers, pain was no stranger to me. Even an encounter with a particular caterpillar that left my hand grotesquely swollen just before taking the PSATs in high school didn't compare to this dental ordeal. This dental emergency not only impacted my physical health but also delivered a harsh financial blow, costing me about $3,000 out-of-pocket. This unexpected expense went straight onto a new health credit line, as I had no emergency fund to cover the cost.

That incident served as a profound awakening for me, making it abundantly clear how an emergency fund could have shielded me from additional debt. Now, with an additional $3,000 owed and future payments looming over me - on top of my rent, motorcycle loan, insurance, and other essential living expenses - the significance of having an emergency fund became painfully evident. This realization propelled me into not only establishing but also maintaining an emergency fund. While I've occasionally dipped into it to manage debt and haven't faced substantial emergencies since its inception, it's comforting knowing it's there.

Now, I maintain a steady $1,000 in my emergency fund, recognizing that while it may not be extensive, it signifies a steadfast step towards financial liberation and stability. My long-term plan, after clearing my debts, is to expand this emergency fund to cover 3-6 months of expenses, further cementing my financial security. The emotional solace that comes with having an emergency fund, reserved exclusively for genuine emergencies, cannot be overstated. This financial buffer gently eases the metaphorical gun away from my head, assuring me that should an unexpected expense arise, I will manage without derailing my budget or lifestyle. This assurance mitigates stress and fosters a more tranquil mental space.

Budgeting has become a pivotal tool in ensuring my emergency fund remains untouched unless a true emergency demands it. I allocate what's needed monthly, and any surplus goes towards managing debt, ensuring that my emergency fund remains intact unless absolutely necessary. The direction this has guided me towards is one where financial stability gradually becomes more tangible, where future planning becomes a bit less daunting and decidedly more feasible. Although I don't utilize specific tools or abide by strict saving amounts, I've found value in utilizing a high-yield savings account to house my emergency fund.

With an API of 4.5%, my high-yield savings account not only keeps my emergency fund secure but also allows it to modestly grow. Once I've successfully navigated out of debt, my plan is to continue to contribute to this account. It will evolve to encompass all of my savings, always maintaining a baseline of $3,000 earmarked for emergencies. This strategy not only fortifies my financial stability but also ensures that I am perpetually prepared to handle unexpected financial demands without compromising my fiscal stability or mental peace.

In a world where fiscal challenges can arise unexpectedly, cultivating a resilient financial future means embracing the power embedded in possessing an emergency fund and adopting consistent saving habits. While $1,000 might be a recommended starting point, the ultimate goal should be to curate an emergency fund substantial enough to cover at least three to six months' worth of living expenses. Establishing and maintaining an emergency fund doesn't merely represent a monetary value but embodies a promise to safeguard one's financial and emotional well-being against the unpredictabilities of life. This is not just about being prepared for unexpected events; it's about creating a stable foundation from which to build a future, free from the looming threat of unmanageable debt and financial instability.

Investing wisely and understanding financial markets

Investing wisely and understanding financial markets are foundational blocks to building a future resistant to the challenges of debt and financial insecurity. Gaining insights into how markets work, appreciating the nuances of various investment vehicles, and understanding the risk associated with each allows us to lay down a path that's not just free of debt but also promising in terms of wealth accumulation. Wise investments are not merely a hedge against future uncertainties but also a tool to cultivate a source of passive income. Yet, as with all things finance-related, investing comes with its own set of challenges and requires a dedicated understanding and a disciplined approach.

My journey into the world of investing began quite early, thanks to my grandmother who not only paid me for helping her out during my high school days but also played a pivotal role in opening a Roth IRA for me. The mechanism was simple, yet powerful - a consistent $50 per week investment that has continued for several years. This early initiation into the principle of 'paying yourself first' and the power of compounding was the first seed sown towards my understanding of investments and financial markets. Furthermore, in line with my knowledge regarding Roth 401k and traditional 401k, as a young person, I always found the Roth variant more fitting. Why? Because you're taxed before you invest, ensuring that the gains you make over the years and decades to follow are yours to enjoy, tax-free, upon retirement.

One perspective that has always stuck with me regarding retirement accounts is treating them not as money, but rather as a kind of tax. I often visualized it as paying a tax into these retirement accounts, which helped me steer clear from viewing it as accessible money. Learning to survive and manage my finances without factoring in my retirement savings taught me disciplined investing, ensuring that I didn't touch it despite the ebbs and flows of life and varying financial scenarios. My investment portfolio isn't just tethered to retirement accounts. I also engaged in a slightly riskier investment avenue, initiating another account wherein I invest $20 per week, venturing into a stock-only portfolio as a short-term experiment.

As a finance major, my academic journey took me deep into the theoretical and analytical aspects of investments. A noteworthy instance from my academic endeavors was an advanced finance class which required us to dig deep into a company's 10K, analyze their tax filings, and essentially dissect their financial stability and stock volatility. While this armed me with the knowledge to assess companies, it also, albeit inadvertently, nudged me into the tumultuous waters of single stock investments, making me realize the value of focusing on the long-term journey rather than quick, risky gains.

Indeed, my maiden venture into investing was a penny stock, SIRI - Sirius XM Radio, to be precise. Although it didn't oscillate much in terms of value, another airline stock I invested in provided me with a lesson on the volatile and unpredictable nature of penny stocks. A lesson in patience, timing, and perhaps a smidgen of luck in investments was learned, albeit the hard way, through these early experiences.

Investing isn't just about watching numbers grow but also about managing and adapting to their fall. Throughout my investment journey, while dealing with debt, I was mindful to manage my investments in a way that provided a fine balance. With one account reserved for retirement and another more flexible account where I invested a modest $20 per week, my strategy was carved out in a way that didn't overextend my finances or jeopardize my debt repayment plan.

During a phase wherein debt played a pivotal role in my financial landscape, I stayed mindful not to overly complicate my investment strategy or overextend myself. My focus was to stabilize my finances, prioritizing debt repayment, and avoiding any additional stress of watching my investment accounts waver in the tempestuous seas of the financial markets. My involvement in crypto and NFTs, while interesting, was brief and insightful, teaching me the merits of thorough research and a measured approach to newer, less understood investment avenues.

Thinking ahead, my long-term goals orbit around consistently fueling my retirement accounts and maximizing the potential of my Health Savings Account (HSA). I see the value in plugging 15% into my retirement account – presently, it's 6% to leverage the company match – knowing that this money will exponentially grow over time thanks to the magic of compounding interest. I am maxing out my HSA, not with the intention of utilizing it in the immediate future but allowing it to act as another investment vehicle, growing and compounding as I age, and thereby, creating a financial safety net for health-related needs in the future.

In regards to the HSA, I've learned that maintaining receipts from health-related expenses over the years can be beneficial. This strategy permits me to pay myself back, tax-free, for those expenses later on, as long as I can provide the necessary documentation. This isn't just about preparing for future financial needs but also creating a robust financial structure that can stand firm against the varying winds of economic change and personal life events.

The path forward, once I am past the realm of debt, does indeed look different. I envision a future where I am not just living within my means, but below it, saving judiciously, and deploying into carefully thought-out investments. Financial freedom is not merely about clearing debt but is also about intelligently managing, deploying, and growing your finances to ensure that the future is not just secure, but also promising in its financial health.

In the grand scheme of things, understanding and navigating the financial markets while investing wisely is akin to charting a course through occasionally turbulent waters. Our experiences, both the victories and the setbacks, form the stepping stones towards crafting a strategy that is resilient, robust, and capable of weathering the financial storms that life might throw our way. It's not merely about accumulating wealth but ensuring that our financial future is steadfast and secure, providing not just for our needs but also facilitating a future that allows for financial peace of mind and security.

Recognizing and resisting consumerist temptations

Navigating through the perils of consumerist temptations necessitates an acute understanding of the pressures that surround everyday spending. From glossy advertisements that showcase an idealized lifestyle to the subtle nudges from our social circles encouraging us to "keep up", the incessant lure towards unnecessary spending can be overwhelming. Yet, recognizing these consumerist temptations and formulating conscious strategies to navigate through them is pivotal in carving a pathway towards a debt-resistant future. Our spending decisions, often colored by a tapestry of internal desires and external influences, can either tether us to a cycle of debt or propel us towards financial stability and freedom.

My journey through the maze of consumerist temptations was both eye-opening and harrowing. The veneer of glossy advertisements and the tantalizing appeal of hot-ticket items, especially limited-release sneakers, left me perpetually vacillating between impulse buys and the impending doom of debt. My mindset was warped by a paradoxical belief that every payday would replenish what was spent, enabling a seemingly endless cycle of spending that perpetually hovered between desire and financial prudence. The urgency created by limited releases and the potential of exorbitant aftermarket prices catalyzed my descent into a whirlwind of purchases, some funded by credit and others by distress sales, all underpinned by a stressful race against accruing interest.

Possessing exclusive items, particularly when they symbolize a particular social or economic status, can be incredibly potent. Often, the scarcity and uniqueness of an item, like those sneakers, dangle before us, offering not just the product, but an entrée into an exclusive club of sorts. The psychology here is particularly manipulative, as it plays on our innate fear of missing out (FOMO) and the human propensity towards wanting to belong and be seen as successful or trendy. But with every impulsive click on the "buy now" button, my financial stability was gradually eroding, placing me precariously on a fiscal cliff that threatened to crumble at any moment.

Yet, amidst the chaos of mismanaged finances and the perpetual chase of the next big thing, a spark of mindfulness began to ignite within me. Budgeting became my beacon of sanity in a sea of unrestrained consumerism. Allocating specific funds towards entertainment or impulsive purchases allowed me to satiate my desires without capsizing my financial ship. The clarity brought about by conscious spending enabled me to delineate between true necessities and fleeting wants, and gradually, the icy grip of consumerist pressures began to thaw.

My newfound financial awareness also illuminated the sheer futility of certain indulgences, such as luxury items or premium travel experiences. My gaze shifted inwards, recognizing that genuine contentment stemmed not from external validations through possessions but from internal peace and satisfaction. My attire, gadgets, and travel choices began reflecting not societal expectations, but my own values and financial priorities. A serendipitous win in a video competition, which furnished me with a plethora of free gear, underscored the realization that true happiness isn't intrinsically tied to relentless spending.

Nonetheless, the shadow of social pressures lingered, often manifesting during social outings and entertainment endeavors. Striking a balance between social enjoyment and financial prudence, especially during bar outings and dinner gatherings, necessitated strategic planning. I found solace and stability in setting tangible boundaries, such as a three-drink maximum, to ensure both my financial and physical wellbeing remained intact. Despite the fleeting temptation to indulge beyond my means, the stark reality of my financial health consistently propelled me back towards restraint and mindfulness.

Online shopping presented its own unique set of challenges, serving up a smorgasbord of desires with a side of instant gratification. The euphoria of adding items to my cart was palpable, yet I learned to navigate through these digital corridors of consumerism without hemorrhaging funds. My strategy was simple yet effective: indulge in the act of virtual shopping, but pause before the final purchase. This pause, sometimes stretching over weeks, allowed the initial fervor to dissipate, often leading to abandoned carts but preserved budgets.

Technology, with its many purchasing platforms and constant influx of promotional deals, exacerbated the challenges of restrained spending. Yet, by converting these digital landscapes into mere windows for browsing rather than portals for impulsive purchasing, I managed to derive visual pleasure without financial pain. While the allure of deals and new products perpetually danced at the periphery of my consciousness, my commitment to debt reduction remained steadfastly in focus, guiding my choices and actions.

In terms of balancing desires and ensuring financial health, my narrative became singularly focused on clawing my way out of debt. Every desire was meticulously weighed against my overarching goal of financial stability, and while the desires remained present, they were often relegated to the backburner, simmering quietly while my financial health took precedence. My engagement with media transformed as well, eschewing product-centric content for financial literacy materials, further solidifying my path towards a debt-free existence.

In my foray into the realm of free-to-play games, I encountered a labyrinth of financial snares. Apex Legends, though ostensibly free, became a costly venture for me. Entranced by the glitz of in-game cosmetic items and the desire to stand out like many others, I found myself shelling out over $2,000 just to don a distinctive avatar and gear. The need to "look cool" in the virtual arena, to belong to an exclusive club of players who sported the latest and most sought-after cosmetic items, was a powerful motivator. However, the ephemeral thrill of these purchases was overshadowed by the weight of the expense and the realization of its superficial nature.

By the time Overwatch 2 rolled around, my experiences with Apex Legends had imparted valuable lessons. I consciously refrained from spending money on in-game items, recognizing that the fleeting pleasure of cosmetic upgrades didn't justify the potential financial strain. Despite the game's allure and the temptations to once again fit into the "cool" bracket with exclusive items, I exercised restraint, keeping my wallet shut. I spent $0 on Overwatch 2, a stark contrast to my prior gaming investments. The evolution in my approach was not merely financial but also psychological – I had come to terms with the fact that I didn't need to purchase virtual items to enjoy a game or to define my place within it.

In retrospect, my dalliance with consumerist temptations has been both a formidable adversary and a formidable teacher. Each misstep, every impulsive purchase, and all moments of financial stress have woven into a tapestry of experiences that have gradually steered me towards a path of mindful spending and financial stability. While the journey has been fraught with challenges, the evolution of my spending habits, forged through trials and tribulations, has become a cornerstone in my pursuit of a debt-resistant future.

Understanding and resisting consumerist temptations isn't merely a financial endeavor; it is deeply intertwined with our psychological frameworks, societal interactions, and personal values. It is about consciously deciphering the myriad of external signals that push towards spending and aligning our financial actions not with fleeting desires but with sustained financial health and stability. The roadmap to a debt-resistant future isn't defined by absolute abstinence from indulgences but by cultivating a harmonious balance where desires are acknowledged yet not permitted to derail our journey towards financial serenity and freedom.

Building a life based on values, not possessions

Building a life centered on values rather than possessions lays a foundation that transcends the transient satisfaction material items bring. This approach shifts the focus towards a deeper, more enduring happiness and fulfillment derived from intrinsic values, relationships, and experiences. This transformation from prioritizing material possessions to valuing non-material elements often stems from introspection and an evaluation of what brings true, lasting contentment. For many, such a shift, whilst challenging, illuminates a path to financial stability by curtailing the accumulation of unnecessary debt, further emphasizing the importance of understanding and adopting this perspective.

In my journey through the labyrinth of values and possessions, a plethora of experiences, some radiant with success and others shadowed by failings, have left an indelible mark on my financial and emotional well-being. There was always a subtle balancing act between values and possessions, and I found myself perpetually teetering on a tightrope of financial management and personal satisfaction. Through the lens of my experiences, there is a poignant realization: the possessions I sought and cherished were never the typical symbols of wealth or status, such as designer clothing or expensive jewelry. Rather, they were items like gadgets, video games, and specific automobiles that held sentimental value and connected with my interests and hobbies.

I've encountered the conundrum of desire versus need, especially in my affection for specific cars: a new Toyota Supra and a 1998 Mazda RX7, each weaving into my life's tapestry through their significance in the anime "Initial D," which was a vibrant part of my growing-up years. These aren't just vehicles; they were nostalgic artifacts, tethering me to cherished memories and experiences. My attachment to these cars wasn't to parade wealth or attain societal approval. Instead, it was a personal affinity, an emotional and historical connection that brought me joy irrespective of external validation.

A pivotal moment that truly reshaped my financial landscape and life priorities was my engagement, a beautiful and momentous occasion that also bestowed upon me a profound realization about financial stability, debt, and future responsibilities. It became imperative for me to shield my future spouse from the financial stress that had long loomed ominously over my head. I found myself staring at a crossroad, with one path leading towards a future haunted by the spectral remains of my debt, and the other towards a future where I could be present, supportive, and financially secure for my family.

In my financial and personal journey, one quote that has profoundly resonated with me and substantially informed my purchasing decisions is: "If someone wasn't looking, would you still buy it?" This succinct yet profound question encourages introspection regarding our buying motives and challenges the pervasive and often subconscious drive to acquire possessions for external validation or societal approval. I fervently believe, and consistently advocate for, the ideology that our purchases should be rooted in personal satisfaction and intrinsic value rather than extrinsically motivated by societal norms, peer pressure, or the perceived judgments of others. The genuine, unadulterated joy derived from a purchase should emanate from its alignment with our personal interests, passions, and values, not from the potential accolades or approval it might garner from external entities. For me, adopting this mindset wasn't merely about redefining my spending habits; it was about reconfiguring my relationship with material possessions and redirecting my financial resources towards items and experiences that offered authentic, personal joy and satisfaction. I encourage others to contemplate this principle in their own spending practices, to discern whether their purchases are reflective of their genuine desires and values, or whether they are subtly or overtly influenced by societal expectations and external perceptions. Through this lens, we can navigate towards a future where our possessions are a true reflection of our selves, rather than a curated display for external consumption, promoting not only financial prudence but also personal authenticity and fulfillment. This philosophy, while seemingly simple, holds the potent ability to divert us from the precipice of debt incurred by purchasing items for mere societal display, steering us towards a more financially stable and emotionally satisfying future.

An overarching theme emerged: I was transitioning from a lifestyle of consuming and spending towards embodying values that prioritized emotional connections, experiences, and financial stability. The engagement, symbolizing a commitment to not just my partner, but also to a future of shared dreams, experiences, and challenges, became a catalyst propelling me towards a more values-oriented life. This shift wasn't merely financial; it permeated through my mental state, emotional well-being, relationships, and overall approach towards life and future aspirations.

These changes steered me towards a life that was simultaneously minimalist and abundant, where the simplicity of possessing less was enriched by the depth of experiences and relationships. The dichotomy of my grandmother's frugality and hard-earned values juxtaposed against my mother's more liberal spending and different value system painted a tableau from which I could draw my own path. It was evident that my values, while molded by my past and family history, needed to be intricately woven with my aspirations, circumstances, and learnings to create a future that resonated with financial, emotional, and relational stability.

The realization that I could derive joy from non-materialistic experiences and connections brought forth a new avenue of happiness and satisfaction. Whether it was spending quality time with my fiancé, exploring new places, or simply enjoying a quiet dinner, the essence of these experiences far outweighed the transient joy of possessions. This revelation was not merely a lifestyle change; it was a life choice that rippled positively through my relationships, emotional well-being, and future aspirations.

My journey towards a values-based life, while deeply personal, is also universally relatable. The oscillation between different sets of values, influenced by generational experiences and personal desires, is a testament to the complexity and uniqueness of every individual's journey towards financial management and personal fulfillment. My grandmother's pragmatism, shaped by her struggles, and my mother's contrasting approach, influenced by her dreams and aspirations, both contributed to my narrative in equal measure. These divergent approaches offered me a palette from which I crafted my own blend of values and financial practices.

Undoubtedly, the echo of past spending habits and the allure of materialistic possessions remain, albeit subdued by the newfound clarity in my values. As I sculpted my values, I unearthed a simple yet profound truth: the things I chose to own, whether material or immaterial, needed to emanate from a space of personal meaning and not from societal expectations or external validations. This change, though it might have been nudged into motion by specific life events, was cultivated and sustained through conscious effort, introspection, and a genuine desire to build a future that was financially stable and emotionally enriching.

In the realm of financial stability and debt management, the nexus between values and possessions becomes glaringly evident. Prioritizing values, especially those that lean towards non-materialistic aspects of life, provides a buffer against impulsive spending, thereby mitigating the accrual of unnecessary debt. It's a strategy that doesn't merely focus on the financial aspect but permeates through various facets of life, enriching relationships, enhancing emotional well-being, and paving the way for a future that isn't tethered by the chains of financial strain.

This narrative isn't just my story. It's a beacon for others navigating through their financial journeys, highlighting the significance of aligning spending and lifestyle choices with deeply-rooted values. This isn't a doctrine but a testament to the peace, stability, and fulfillment that arises when one's life is constructed around intrinsic values rather than external, material possessions. Building a life that mirrors our authentic selves, unfettered by the societal norms and pressures, allows for a future that's not only financially stable but also emotionally rewarding and true to our deepest desires and aspirations. It's a potent antidote to a debt-ridden future, illuminating a path that promises not just financial peace, but a life that is genuinely rich in experiences, relationships, and personal fulfillment.

CONCLUSION

Reflecting on the journey of understanding debt

Delving into a reflection on understanding debt, one cannot help but consider how this financial instrument, designed initially as a mechanism to facilitate enhanced economic activity and opportunity, has morphed into a tool that, if mishandled, can exert an almost tyrannical control over one's life and choices. It's like an omnipresent specter, subtly influencing decisions and infiltrating dreams with a relentless persistence. The journey of comprehending and navigating debt, particularly in a culture that so effortlessly entwines it with aspirational living, is one fraught with challenges, learnings, and unexpected revelations.

My own path towards understanding debt started out with blissful ignorance, where I was merely a participant in a societal norm that I had neither questioned nor understood in depth. I was ensnared by the glamorous portrayals of lifestyles I couldn't afford but was convinced I deserved, all because media and pop culture subtly embedded the belief that indulgence today could be painlessly paid for tomorrow. My personal, initially unconstrained journey through a world of buying and owing illustrates a common trajectory, where the immediate joy of acquisition overshadows the lingering obligation of repayment.

The haunting realization that every purchase on credit was not merely a transaction but an ongoing commitment that would persistently nibble at my financial stability was an awakening that evolved gradually. Every seemingly inconsequential purchase accumulated, morphing into a staggering mountain of obligation that loomed ominously over each financial decision, each life choice. And then, the subtle yet incessant stress, the persistent worry that accompanies being in debt, began to weave its way through my days and nights, casting a shadow that was often intangible yet perpetually present.

Navigating through this understanding, I was compelled to unravel the intricate threads that had woven the web in which I was entangled. This meant understanding not just the tangible numerical aspect of debt, but the psychological, emotional, and social facets that had silently coaxed me into this predicament. Why had I bought things I didn't need? What void was I attempting to fill with every click of the 'purchase' button? It was a journey that demanded introspection, accountability, and an honest confrontation with not just my spending habits, but the underlying motivations and insecurities that propelled them.

At some point, amidst the chaos of numbers and overdue notices, I started to see the amalgamation of choices that had led me to this point. It wasn't just about buying things; it was about the illusion of fulfillment, the temporary inoculation against dissatisfaction, and the desire to mirror the lifestyles that were so prominently displayed across various media. Each purchase was a silent scream for acceptance, a plea for acknowledgment in a world that often seemed to measure worth by material possession and aesthetic presentation.

Resilience, I learned, was an unanticipated ally on this journey. As I scrutinized my relationship with money, spending, and debt, a newfound strength emerged from the rubble of my previously mishandled finances. I learned to say 'no', not just to purchases but to the pervasive belief that my value was intrinsically linked to my possessions. I learned that resisting the lure of immediate gratification, in pursuit of long-term financial stability and freedom, was a triumph, albeit one that was often quietly celebrated in the solitude of my own conscience.

This transcendence from being submerged in a quagmire of debt to gradually lifting my head above its suffocating embrace was not linear. It was punctuated by setbacks, moments of weakness, and the occasional relapse into old habits. Yet, each misstep became a stepping stone, a lesson that silently steered me towards not just financial recovery, but an evolved understanding of my own drivers, vulnerabilities, and true needs.

Embracing frugality, once perceived as a limitation, emerged as an unexpected liberation. Unshackling myself from the constant need to acquire, to demonstrate worth through material accumulation, I discovered a peace and stability that had eluded me even during times of extravagant spending. I learned that living within my means was not a punishment, but a path that led towards genuine financial freedom, unperturbed by the incessant anxiety that debt inevitably bequeaths.

In hindsight, every struggle, every moment of despair that was intrinsically intertwined with my journey through debt, imparted invaluable lessons that have reshaped my values, choices, and future trajectory. The path, albeit strewn with challenges and moments of despair, fortuitously directed me towards not merely an improved financial situation, but a profound reevaluation of what truly matters, what genuinely brings joy, peace, and stability.

Concluding this chapter, it is clear that debt, while being a tangible financial burden, is also emblematic of deeper, often unexplored personal and societal issues. It's not merely about money owed; it's about understanding why it was borrowed in the first place, confronting the beliefs, desires, and insecurities that facilitated this choice, and ultimately, charting a path forward that acknowledges these facets, utilizing them as guideposts towards not just fiscal, but holistic well-being.

In a society that so often subtly equates worth with wealth and social standing with spending, choosing a path of restraint, frugality, and prudent financial management is inherently an act of rebellion. It is a choice that not only propels one towards financial stability but also necessitates the deconstruction of ingrained beliefs and the reconstruction of a life that, while perhaps less ostentatious, is authentically one's own.

A journey through understanding debt is, in essence, a journey through understanding oneself. It's about unraveling the complex web of personal and societal beliefs, emotions, and motivations that have influenced financial decisions and forging a path that, while acknowledging these elements, is not dictated by them. The shadow of debt, while initially ominous, can inadvertently illuminate a path towards not just financial recovery, but personal discovery, evolution, and eventual liberation.

Reiterating the importance of compassion and understanding for those in debt

In a society often emblematic of consumerism and financial success, understanding and compassion towards those struggling with debt can sometimes be overshadowed by a harsher, more judgmental perspective. This stark dichotomy between the lived experiences of those dealing with debt and the broader societal narrative, especially in media portrayals and social circles, necessitates a profound reflection on the emotional and psychological toll that such financial stress can exert. In the trajectory towards fostering a more empathetic society, reiterating the importance of understanding and compassion for individuals grappling with debt becomes indispensable.

Navigating through the murky waters of debt is not merely a financial journey; it is an emotionally taxing ordeal that often silently permeates every aspect of one's life. The psychological burden, the silent stress that invariably accompanies financial strife, is a nuanced, multi-faceted challenge that can quietly erode mental and emotional wellbeing. Reflecting on this, one cannot help but realize that an empathetic, non-judgmental understanding from the wider society can act as a much-needed respite, a silent acknowledgment that while they may be financially encumbered, they are not emotionally isolated.

Delving into this further, it is vital to recognize that every individual's journey with debt is unique, influenced by a myriad of factors that may not always be overtly visible. This complexity, this nuanced tapestry that intertwines financial choices with emotional responses, social pressures, and psychological wellbeing, necessitates a compassionate approach that seeks to understand, rather than hastily judge or condemn.

"I remember the isolation," becomes a silent whisper in my introspective moments, recalling those times when the weight of my debt felt simultaneously crushing and shamefully hidden. For years, I navigated through the highs of acquisition and the lows of persistent obligation, all while meticulously curating a facade that bore little resemblance to my financial reality. And it wasn't merely about the tangible burden of repayment, it was the silent, often overlooked emotional and psychological strain that invariably intertwined with every overdue notice, every unopened bill.

A peculiar solitude often accompanies financial struggle, especially in a culture that extols financial success and subtly intertwines it with personal worth. I often found myself oscillating between a desperate desire to confess my fiscal missteps and the paralyzing fear of judgment, of being perceived as irresponsible, impulsive, or financially inept. It was a solitary journey, where my smiles masked a silent anxiety and my acquisitions concealed a burgeoning, omnipresent financial strain.

In those moments, when the disparity between my portrayed life and lived reality was most stark, compassion and understanding from those around me would have been a soothing balm, a gentle acknowledgment that my worth was not defined by my financial stability, nor my character by my debt. Yet, the fear of judgment, the potential for condescension or pity, perpetually silenced my confessions, compelling me to navigate through the tumultuous journey of debt in isolating solitude.

It's this intrinsic understanding, this personal acquaintance with the silent struggle that accompanies financial burden, that propels my advocacy for compassion and understanding towards those in similar predicaments. Because debt is not merely a numerical problem to be solved. It is an emotional, psychological, and social challenge that requires an approach that acknowledges these multifaceted dimensions.

Unveiling this further, empathy towards those struggling with debt is not merely about providing a non-judgmental ear, but also about fostering an environment where financial struggles can be openly discussed, without fear of stigmatization or condemnation. It is about extending a hand, not merely in assistance but in understanding, recognizing that the path of financial management is one that is often punctuated by missteps, challenges, and unexpected hurdles.

This compassionate approach becomes not merely a supportive framework but an essential foundation upon which constructive, effective strategies for managing and overcoming debt can be built. It shifts the narrative from one of isolation and shame to one of collective support and empowering guidance, where individuals are not defined by their financial struggles, but acknowledged for their courage in confronting and navigating through them.

In essence, emphasizing the importance of compassion and understanding towards those in debt underscores a broader, more inclusive perspective, one that recognizes the multi-dimensional nature of financial struggles and seeks to provide not just pragmatic solutions but emotional and psychological support. It is a call to action, to shift the societal narrative from judgment and presumption to empathy and support, fostering an environment where individuals can navigate through their financial challenges with dignity, respect, and an empowering sense of community.

In a landscape where financial stability is often heralded as a symbol of success and autonomy, compassionately acknowledging the silent struggle, the often invisible emotional and psychological burden of those dealing with debt, becomes an invaluable step towards fostering a society that champions collective wellbeing, support, and understanding, ensuring that no one has to navigate through their financial journey in isolating, judgmental solitude.

In this narrative, compassion becomes more than empathy; it becomes a silent ally in the journey towards financial stability, providing a safe, supportive space where individuals can navigate through their debt without the added burden of societal judgment, stigma, or isolation. It becomes a catalyst for change, for evolving the conversation around debt from one of blame and failure to one of understanding, support, and collective empowerment.

Encouraging societal change and improved financial education

As we traverse through the myriad of experiences, stories, and lessons that the specter of debt has thrown into the limelight, there's a reflective pause that allows us to ponder, not only on individual experiences but also on the collective societal approach towards debt and financial management. A pervasive theme that continually surfaces is the palpable need for a twofold change: a societal shift in perspectives towards debt and those ensnared by it, as well as an enhanced emphasis on financial education that equips individuals with the tools to navigate the often treacherous waters of financial management.

Considering the former, encouraging a societal shift, particularly in perspectives towards debt and financial management, necessitates a profound reevaluation of prevalent narratives and stereotypes. Far too often, those grappling with debt are swiftly, and often unjustly, labeled with stigmas related to irresponsibility or impulsivity. This all-too-common narrative perpetuates a cycle of judgment and isolation, hindering constructive conversations and potential support systems that could foster healthier financial management and mental wellbeing.

Understanding the need for improved financial education demands a reflective look at the current landscape of financial knowledge and resources available to diverse populations. For many, navigating through the complex world of finances – with its credit scores, interest rates, and varied loan types – becomes an intricate dance, one that is often learned through trial and, unfortunately, error. The provision of accessible, comprehensible, and practical financial education becomes a pivotal stepping stone in equipping individuals to manage their finances adeptly and make informed decisions.

Reflecting on my personal journey through the maze of debt, it becomes glaringly apparent how a lack of comprehensive financial education significantly impacted my financial choices and strategies. There were numerous instances when I found myself floundering, trying to discern the intricacies of interest rates, debt consolidation, and credit scores, often learning through the unforgiving lens of hindsight. My understanding of financial management was essentially a patchwork of information, cobbled together through personal experiences and often, through the consequences of missteps.

This poignant understanding that arises from personal experiences reinforces the imperative nature of ensuring that financial education becomes an accessible, foundational aspect of learning. I recall moments when an understanding of the complexities of credit card interest or the implications of loan deferrals could have dramatically altered my financial choices, propelling me towards more sustainable, informed decisions. It's an acknowledgment that resonates, not merely as a retrospective wish but as a forward-looking necessity, ensuring that future generations are equipped with the knowledge to navigate their financial journeys adeptly.

Moreover, my experiences amplify the silent, yet pervasive role that societal perspectives play in shaping our financial narratives. There were countless instances when the fear of judgment or the stigma associated with debt silently influenced my choices, often deterring me from seeking help or discussing my financial predicaments openly. This silent struggle, this isolating journey through financial management, underscores the imperative need to shift societal perceptions, fostering an environment that encourages open dialogue, support, and collective empowerment.

Navigating through the turbulent waters of debt was, for me, often an isolating, solitary journey, one where the fear of judgment perpetually lingered in the shadows. A palpable shift in societal perspectives, one that fosters empathy, understanding, and support, would have transformed this journey, providing not merely a safe space to discuss and navigate through financial challenges, but also facilitating a collective, societal approach towards healthier financial management.

Simultaneously, embarking on a journey towards improved financial education demands a collective, inclusive approach, ensuring that individuals from varied demographics, socio-economic statuses, and age groups are provided with the resources, knowledge, and support to manage their finances adeptly. It necessitates a strategic amalgamation of practical knowledge, accessible resources, and ongoing support, ensuring that financial education becomes a lifelong journey, one that evolves to meet the unique, changing needs of diverse populations.

Encouraging societal change and improved financial education thus surfaces as a collective call to action, beckoning society to foster a two-pronged approach that shifts perspectives towards empathy and understanding, while simultaneously ensuring that comprehensive, practical financial education becomes accessible to all. It is an approach that doesn't merely seek to address the symptoms of financial mismanagement but aims to transform the foundational narratives and structures that define our financial journeys, ensuring that they are characterized by understanding, knowledge, and collective empowerment.

In this reflective pause, there emerges a clarity, not merely of the challenges and struggles that permeate the journey through debt, but also of the potential pathways through which society can evolve towards healthier, more supportive financial narratives. It is a clarity that emanates from the interwoven threads of personal experiences and broader societal structures, coalescing into a comprehensive understanding that compassion, knowledge, and collective empowerment form the triad that propels us towards transformative, societal change.

It's a change that doesn't merely seek to provide symptomatic relief but aims to transform the foundational structures, perspectives, and narratives that define our financial journeys, ensuring that they are pathways characterized by empathy, understanding, and empowered, informed choices. And as this transformative journey unfolds, it illuminates the potential for a future where the journey through debt and financial management becomes not an isolating, stigmatized struggle, but a collective, empowered pathway towards financial wellbeing, support, and collective empowerment.

Emphasizing the possibility and hope for a debt-free life

Navigating through the conundrum of financial matters, where debt frequently looms like an unyielding shadow, there often emerges a beacon of light, symbolizing hope, possibility, and the prospect of a debt-free life. While the journey towards financial solvency often appears steeped in complexity and challenges, it's essential to underscore the potential that resides in strategic financial management, informed decisions, and consistent, disciplined approaches towards debt repayment and financial planning. The quest for a debt-free life, while punctuated with its unique challenges, simultaneously opens up avenues for exploration, learning, and ultimately, financial liberation.

Hope, a word often used lightly, carries profound weight when placed against the backdrop of financial adversity and the struggles associated with debt. It's not merely a passive aspiration but a dynamic, motivating force that propels individuals towards strategic action, careful planning, and the relentless pursuit of financial stability. Hope becomes the fuel that energizes the journey towards a debt-free life, inspiring individuals to explore possibilities, formulate strategies, and persistently pursue their financial goals, even amidst challenges and setbacks.

Delving into my own narrative and the intricate journey through the landscapes of debt, I've grappled with the pervasive influence of financial burdens, felt the weight of mounting debts, and encountered the myriad emotions that accompany financial struggles. The spectrum of experiences, from moments of despair to sparks of hope, have been inextricably interwoven into my financial journey, painting a vivid tapestry that illustrates not merely the struggles, but also the possibilities that emerge even amidst financial adversity.

I remember staring at the numbers, a sea of figures that symbolized the debts that loomed ominously over my financial landscape. The emotions that ebbed and flowed through me were a kaleidoscope, ranging from despair and frustration to a quiet, persistent whisper of hope that refused to be silenced. This whisper, this subtle, yet unyielding voice, became a constant companion, gently nudging me towards exploration, learning, and the gradual formulation of a strategy that aimed to navigate through and eventually, emerge from the abyss of debt.

Hope became more than just a concept; it transformed into a tangible, actionable pathway that paved the way towards financial solvency. I learned to explore, to seek knowledge, to understand the intricacies of debt management, and to formulate a strategic approach that aligned with my unique financial situation and goals. I understood that the path towards a debt-free life wasn't merely a distant possibility, but a realistic goal that could be achieved through informed decisions, strategic planning, and consistent, disciplined action.

This journey was punctuated with its unique challenges and learning curves. I encountered setbacks, navigated through unexpected financial hurdles, and grappled with the complexities that characterize the journey towards debt repayment and financial management. Yet, amidst these challenges, hope remained a steadfast companion, not merely as a passive wish but as an active, motivating force that propelled me towards continued action, learning, and strategic financial management.

The intertwining of hope and strategy became a pivotal aspect of my journey towards financial stability. I understood that hope wasn't merely about wishful thinking, but about combining aspirations with actionable strategies, aligning dreams with realistic plans, and intertwining visions of a debt-free future with the pragmatic, day-to-day actions that propel towards financial solvency.

The realm of possibilities that unfold once hope is strategically intertwined with actionable planning and disciplined action is vast and encompassing. It unveils the potential to transform financial narratives, to shift from a path characterized by debt and financial struggle to one that embodies financial stability, empowerment, and freedom. The journey towards a debt-free life, while undeniably challenging, opens up vistas for exploration, learning, and the realization of financial goals and aspirations.

The personal journey through debt, with its intricacies, challenges, and the amalgamation of struggles and triumphs, exemplifies the pervasive potential that resides in each individual's path towards financial stability. It underscores the possibility that even amidst the complexities and challenges that punctuate the path, there emerges a potential for learning, growth, and the ultimate realization of financial liberation and stability.

Hope and strategy thus become the intertwined forces that propel individuals towards the realization of their financial goals and the pursuit of a debt-free life. It illustrates that even amidst the challenges, setbacks, and unexpected hurdles that characterize the journey, there resides an unyielding potential for transformation, for the strategic realization of financial goals, and for the actualization of a life free from the shadows of debt.

Navigating through my own financial narrative, understanding the intricacies of debt management, and experiencing firsthand the impact of strategic, disciplined action towards debt repayment, the possibility of a debt-free life does not merely remain a distant dream. It transforms into a tangible, achievable reality, achievable through the amalgamation of hope, informed decisions, strategic planning, and consistent, disciplined action. It becomes a testament to the potential that resides within each individual's financial journey, illuminating the pathways towards financial stability, empowerment, and liberation.

The reflection upon these pathways, upon the possibilities, challenges, and triumphs that characterize the journey towards a debt-free life, provides not merely a retrospective understanding but also propels forward-looking momentum. It becomes a catalyst that fosters continuous learning, strategic action, and the persistent pursuit of financial goals, ensuring that the journey towards financial stability and freedom becomes an achievable, realistic pathway, attainable through the intertwining of hope, strategy, and disciplined, consistent action.

In conclusion, while the road towards a debt-free existence can be tumultuous, marked with unexpected obstacles and learning curves, it's also sprinkled with moments of triumph over past mistakes and newly acquired wisdom. My journey through the quagmire of debt into the realms of stability and financial tranquility has been equally arduous and enlightening. It's a journey that doesn't merely navigate through the complexities of debt management but traverses towards a future characterized by financial stability, empowerment, and the endless possibilities that emerge when financial freedom is realized.

A call to action: Empowering oneself and others to take control of their financial destiny

As we embark on this final leg of our explorative journey through the multifaceted domain of debt and financial management in "Debt has a gun to my head", we find ourselves standing on the precipice of empowerment and action. Navigating through the terrains of debt, exploring the myriad emotions, challenges, and learning curves that characterize this journey, we inevitably arrive at a pivotal juncture, where knowledge and understanding morph into the catalysts for action, empowerment, and the strategic management of our financial futures.

A vital component of empowerment stems from a deeply ingrained acknowledgment of autonomy and control over one's financial destiny. It pivots on the awareness that, while our financial journeys may be punctuated with challenges, setbacks, and unexpected hurdles, we simultaneously wield the capacity to learn, adapt, and strategically navigate through these complexities towards the realization of our financial goals and aspirations.

Treading upon my own path through the convoluted world of debt and financial management, I was invariably confronted with a multitude of emotions, challenges, and decisions. The path, often strewn with unexpected obstacles and learning curves, simultaneously unveiled vistas for exploration, understanding, and ultimately, the formulation of strategic approaches towards managing and eventually, eliminating debt.

In my journey, I often found myself ensnared in the complexities and challenges that characterize debt. I grappled with feelings of frustration, anxiety, and at times, a pervasive sense of despair as I navigated through the intricacies of financial management, debt repayment, and strategic planning. Yet, intertwined within these emotions and experiences, there emerged a steadfast, unyielding glimmer of hope, empowerment, and the persistent pursuit of financial stability and freedom.

It was an intrinsic belief in the possibility of change, of transformation, and the potential to alter my financial trajectory that became a constant, unwavering companion throughout my journey. It propelled me to seek knowledge, to understand the nuances of financial management, to explore various strategies for debt repayment, and to invariably take control of my financial destiny, steering it towards stability, empowerment, and liberation.

Through the variegated experiences of navigating through debt, of encountering challenges, and subsequently formulating and implementing strategies towards financial management, I realized the pervasive power and potential that resides in each of our financial journeys. I learned that empowerment is not merely a conceptual aspiration but a tangible, achievable goal that can be realized through knowledge, strategic action, and the persistent, disciplined pursuit of our financial objectives.

Empowering oneself and others to take control of their financial destinies involves an amalgamation of knowledge, strategy, and action. It entails equipping oneself with the knowledge and understanding necessary to navigate through the intricacies of financial management, formulating strategic approaches towards debt repayment and financial planning, and subsequently implementing these strategies through consistent, disciplined action.

This empowerment does not merely reside in the realm of personal financial management but extends into the broader spectrum of societal understanding, compassion, and collective empowerment. It involves fostering an environment that encourages learning, exploration, and the sharing of knowledge and experiences, enabling collective growth, understanding, and the communal pursuit of financial stability and freedom.

Envisioning a future characterized by financial stability, empowerment, and the absence of debt, becomes not merely a personal aspiration but a collective goal. It transforms into a shared journey, where experiences, knowledge, and strategies are communally shared, fostering an environment that propels each individual towards their unique financial goals while simultaneously nurturing a collective movement towards societal financial stability and empowerment.

As we meander towards the conclusion of this narrative and reflective exploration of debt, financial management, and empowerment, let us carry forward the knowledge, experiences, and insights gained throughout this journey. Let it fuel our paths towards financial stability, empower our actions, and inspire a collective movement towards widespread financial knowledge, understanding, and empowerment.

To every reader who has accompanied me on this explorative journey through the realms of debt, financial struggle, and ultimately, empowerment and liberation, I extend a heartfelt thank you. Your engagement, your willingness to explore, understand, and journey through these narratives, not merely as passive observers but as active participants in a collective movement towards financial stability and freedom, is deeply appreciated.

In closing, the shared stories, insights, and explorations throughout "Debt has a gun to my head" seek to inspire not merely contemplative reflection but active, strategic, and empowered action. Let us carry forward these insights, knowledge, and experiences as we navigate through our unique financial paths, propelling ourselves towards our financial goals, and fostering a collective environment of knowledge, empowerment, and the communal pursuit of a future free from the shadows of debt.

Thank you, dear reader, for traversing this path with me, for exploring the landscapes of debt, challenges, empowerment, and hope, and for becoming an intrinsic component of this collective journey towards financial understanding, management, and liberation. May this journey inspire, empower, and strategically guide each of us towards our unique financial aspirations and collectively, towards a future characterized by widespread financial stability, empowerment, and freedom.

Index

A

B

C

D

E

O

P

R

S

T

U

ABOUT THE AUTHOR

Sanish Shrestha is a proud first-generation American, born and raised in Fort Worth, TX. From his early years, Sanish was captivated by the allure of California, a dream inspired by cherished trips to visit his aunt and fueled by his love for all things Disney. Today, he calls California home, having realized that childhood aspiration.

Sanish is an alumnus of the University of San Francisco, where he earned a degree in finance. Although his academic pursuits centered on finance, life had a different plan. An unexpected opportunity in construction management led him to his current role in project management for an electrical manufacturer. His time at the university, while not directly related to his current profession, provided a foundation that opened doors into the workforce, helping him find his niche.

However, the journey wasn't without its challenges. Over the years, Sanish grappled with the seductive pull of debt and the temptations of lifestyle inflation. A decade after leaving his hometown and half a decade post-college, he took control of his finances. This book is a testament to that journey. It chronicles his experiences with debt, the lessons learned, and his determined path to financial freedom. It's not just a guide but a reflection of a pivotal moment in Sanish's life—a time of transformation and growth.

For more information or to connect with Sanish, please send a message though Linkedin
https://www.linkedin.com/in/sanishkshrestha/